FAITH

FULL

A Practical Guide For FULLY
Living Out Your Faith

Drew Froese
www.drewfroese.com

Please purchase books at store.bookbaby.com *FAITH FULL*

For more information on Drew, to follow his blog,
or to book a speaking engagement visit: www.drewfroese.com

First Edition

Cover design by Drew Froese

Self-Published using Book Baby by Drew Froese
www.drewfroese.com

Ordering information:
For details, contact drewfroese@outlook.com
Or purchase at store.bookbaby.com *FAITH FULL*
Print ISBN: 978-1-09836-800-5
eBook ISBN: 978-1-09836-801-2

Printed in the United States of America

Dedication

To My Bride

Who am I to be so blessed to call you my wife?

I love you!

Contents

PART THREE
Drive the Truck
(Applying What You've Learned)

Introduction

More

Monday – Friday

6:00 – Wake up

6:08 – Actually wake up

6:30 – Pour first cup of coffee and sit down for some quiet time…maybe

7:00 – Finish breakfast, remembering an eighth of what I read

7:05 – Wake up the kids who, despite doing this every morning, try to convince me they "just can't get up"

7:30 – Hurry off to work

6:30 – Get home from work and kids' activities. Eat dinner.

7:30 – Put kids to bed

7:40 – Put kids to bed again

7:50 – PUT kids to bed AGAIN

8:00 – Discuss inventions that would prevent the kids from getting out of bed

11:30 – Go to bed.

11:31 – Regret staying up this late

11:32 or 12:15 or 1:00 – Fall asleep

Saturday

Sleep in less than I had hoped

Run errands

Run the kids to _____

Get things done around the house.

Sunday

Sit in church.

Be inspired to live boldly for Christ

Go home

Repeat.

How often have you looked at your life and longed for more—a deeper relationship with God, a richer, bolder faith, a larger eternal impact? How often have you been discouraged by the loop in which you find yourself? A loop that has life on repeat, drowning out the "life to the fullest" that Jesus came to give. Whether you can relate to the previous example, or you have your own "repeat", as a pastor, I've seen this discouraging pattern all too often. This may surprise you, but I don't just see it in others; I see it in myself. As I read the Bible, I'm inspired by disciples who shared their faith boldly, spreading the message of Christ in the face of punishment and death, confidently living out their faith. I know that Jesus commanded His followers to love deeply and share His Good News. When I read about the early church and the devotion of Christians throughout history, I yearn to live with just an ounce of their courage and faith.

To the core of my being, I know I was created to make an impact for God's Kingdom. Despite being convinced of this truth, sadly, there is often a disconnect between the longing in my soul and what my life actually looks like. I fall into the repeat pattern that has my faith moving at an embarrassingly slow crawl, my life poorly reflecting an all-powerful, all-loving God.

Is this true for you? Do you find yourself in this loop? The cycles of life quieting the brave, transformative, community-impacting Christianity that you long for? Do you desire to fully live out your faith? Do you wish you had the tools to stop the loop and get after it? Do you want more?

My guess is your answers to all those are, "Yes!" Although the disconnect between your longing and your life may be frustrating, let me encourage you with this. Don't let the frustration diminish your pursuit of more; let it stoke a passion to fight against the loop, to fight for the 'more' you desire. God's plan for your life is not ho-hum, get enough gold stars of church attendance to make it to heaven. God wants a deeper relationship with you. He wants you to grow in your confidence in His love. God wants your life to show the world His sacrificial love, full of grace and truth. He wants your relationships to be healthy and vibrant. God wants your brokenness restored. He wants you to experience the joy of following Him. God knows that when you deepen your love and trust in Him, obediently submitting to His will, the 'more' that you're hoping for will turn into the 'more' that you experience.

This Isn't Going To Be Easy

Desiring your faith to grow, and knowing God wants your faith to grow, doesn't mean fully living out your faith is going to be easy. This isn't to discourage you, but to prepare you for a journey of endurance. Even though I hate math, I wish the knowledge of how to fully live out my faith was like solving a math problem. Tell me what the formula is, I'll do it, and then I'll have a more robust faith. Instead, fully living out your faith is a life-long process of trials, setbacks, and growth. Theologian and pastor A.W. Tozer affirms this refrain, "I have often wished there were some ways to bring modern Christians into a deeper spiritual life painlessly by short easy lessons; but such wishes are in vain... No shortcuts exist!"[1]

> *God's plan for your life is not ho-hum, get enough gold stars of church attendance to make it to heaven...He wants you to experience the joy of following Him.*

When discouragement arises, it's helpful to remember that Jesus promises to be with you (see Mt. 28:20), and God's Word promises that the Holy Spirit will give you the strength you need (see Eph. 1:17-20). These verses don't promise it will be easy. In fact, Jesus warns that following Him will come with great difficulties (see Jn. 15:20). Know it's going to be trying, but never forget the challenge and reassurance of Jesus in the book of Matthew:

"Then Jesus said to his disciples, 'If any of you wants to be my follower, you must give up your own way, take up your cross, and follow me. If you try to hang on to your life, you will lose it. But if you give up your life for my sake, you will save it. And what do you benefit if you gain the whole world but lose your own soul? Is anything worth more than your soul?" (16:24-26)

Fully living out your faith is a high calling. It means you must "give up your life," but this

> *Fully living out your faith is a high calling. It means you must "give up your life," but this high calling comes with a priceless promise, "you will save it."*

high calling comes with a priceless promise, "you will save it." Jesus is essentially saying, "You know all that stuff that I'm asking you to give up to follow me? All that stuff that you feel like you can't live without? All those things that might make this tough? Those are nothing compared to the value of your soul and the value of what you get if you follow me: You get true life!"

Jesus is calling His disciples (and you) to give up what you think is of great value for something of eternally better value. The life and hope Jesus offers to those who follow Him are supremely superior to the difficulty that following Him will bring. It may be much easier to coast through life, ignoring the longing in your heart and the calling of God, but deep down inside, that's not what you want…that's not what God wants. If you give up on fully living out your faith because it is difficult, you will miss out on the bigger, better, eternal reality of joy (see Jn. 15:11), rewards (see Lk. 6:22-23), rest (see Mt. 11:28), peace (see Jn. 16:33), and living life to the fullest (see Jn. 10:10). As you gather tools and are challenged to fully live out your faith, keep these promises in mind because it will be tough, but it will absolutely be worth it.

What Do You Want More Of?

Throughout this book, your understanding of how to read the Bible, how to engage in spiritual disciplines, spiritual gifts, and how to serve, mentor, and evangelize will increase. Each chapter shows you the importance of these elements,

> *It will be tough, but it will absolutely be worth it.*

inspiring you and giving you tools to integrate into your life. By the end of your reading, you will have a wealth of information that will allow you to develop and deepen your faith. As exciting as this is, and as eager as I am to help you fully live out your faith, there is a danger that I need to address before we go any further. The danger is exposed with an honest response to this question: What do you want more of?

Reading this book may have you dismissing the question with this answer: "Obviously, I want to fully live out my faith." I want to caution you not to ignore the question with this quick, easy answer. Here's why: Just reading a book that gives you an understanding of ways to fully live out your faith does not equate to fully living out your faith (see Jas 2:14-20). You will never move to fully living out your faith if all you do is gain knowledge of 'how to', without putting 'how to' into practice.

An honest answer to the question "What do you want more of?" will not be answered by how your mouth responds, but by how you incorporate these practices into your life. This book is not written to make you an expert in your knowledge of how to deepen your faith. It is

> *An honest answer to the question "What do you want more of?" will not be answered by how your mouth responds, but by how you integrate these practices into your life.*

here to give you guidance and tools to implement so that you can become more like Christ. I pray that this book will equip you to live out your faith in a way where your action and attitudes look more like Jesus. I pray it helps you engage in a richer relationship with God, creating a greater experience of the fruit of God's Spirit: love, joy, peace, patience, kindness, goodness, faithfulness, gentleness, and self-control.

As your faith becomes fuller, I hope your growth affects how you interact with everyone in your life, leading to better relationships. I long for you to see the world in new colors of God's goodness. I pray that this book gives you the tools to draw close to God's heart, a heart that breaks for those who don't know Him. Correctly approaching this book should move you to elevating your interaction with God, cultivating a selfless, pursuing love that moves you to serve and love those around you with a heart impassioned to show God's grace. If all this is the 'more' you want, turn the page, keep reading, and be prepared for the thrilling journey that awaits.

Questions For Reflection:

- In what you just read, what resonates most strongly with you? Why?
- What is the most challenging part of living out your faith?
- What are some areas about your faith with which you are unsatisfied or which you want more?
- What are your most significant barriers to growth (i.e., busyness, lack of motivation)? How can you overcome those barriers as you read this book?

PART ONE

The Fuel To Live

If you own a car, you spend approximately seven to ten hours every year filling it with gas. Seven to ten hours standing next to your vehicle, trying to predict what the final amount will be, getting inundated with the gas station news (which always seems to be a week behind).

A few years ago, a company called "Filld" was started to offer the convenience of gas, delivered to your car as you sleep. Everyone who relies on a car needs gas, and who wants to spend any time at a gas station? What a great solution.

Wouldn't it be incredible if there was a similar product offered for other areas of your life? Wouldn't it be fantastic if your faith could grow in a similar way? Sadly, many people treat their interaction with God with the same lens of convenience.

Perhaps church is the sole way your faith is "filled." With the increase of online viewership, many people's only interaction with God is when His Word is delivered through a screen. This isn't just a problem for online interaction. Some have treated church attendance in the same way— "Just fill me up, pastor, and let me get on until my tank is depleted."

Whether or not these approaches to faith define you, this section will give you the tools and motivation to engage in God's primary way of filling your engine. The church and your pastor do play a role, but my hope is you will realize and apply the regular practice of inputting God's Word, not merely waiting for someone else to fill your tank.

Chapter 1

Transformative Bible Reading

When my twin brother and I turned 18, my parents treated the entire family to the most elegant dining experience of our lives. We were going to a highly rated, very expensive French restaurant. As we dressed in our best clothes, I recalled statements made earlier in the day about escargot. I was thrilled to try the food at a fancy restaurant, but my anticipation also came with a fear of all the interesting items I may have to try, flavors my palate was not accustomed to. Upon arriving and being seated, my Dad said he would be the only one who needed a menu as he would order for us all. When the waiter served the food, I hesitantly sampled some of the more unique offerings. I was underwhelmed. Sure, the things I tried were delicious, but with the amount of money my Dad was spending, I expected something life changing.

Then something significant happened. The chef came to our table, introduced himself, and began explaining how he had compiled each dish on the table. He answered questions, shared his history of cooking and his passion for what he does. This conversation completely changed the dining experience. What I was eating was transformed from merely expensive, fancy food into an expression of intimacy, intentionality, and creativity from the chef to me. Our conversation with the chef made me realize there is more going on with my food than ordering, cooking, and eating.

Yes, all those things happened, but hearing about the chef's preparation, how he thinks about the food, how he takes certain spices to prepare it "just right" helped me appreciate and savor the dining experience in a more profound way. It allowed me to taste the food's unique design, and I was able to know the chef, which helped me consume the food (even the escargot) with greater appreciation.

This rare interaction points directly to how you can interact with God and God's Word. You can read His Word to get information to help make decisions in life, or you can allow your encounter with God to transform the way you engage in His Word, realizing it's more than just information on a page. It's the "chef's" communication with you.

God uses the Bible to communicate with you about the way things should be, about His love for you, and about what He has done, is doing, and will do to restore creation to the original, perfect environment He meant it to be. The Bible is not just history; it's His story. The Bible is the primary

> *God uses the Bible to communicate with you about the way things should be, about His love for you, and about what He has done, is doing, and will do to restore creation to the original, perfect environment He meant it to be.*

way God invites you to know Him more, revealing why you should devote your life to following Him. The Bible is less like a menu and more like a love letter. The more you learn to know God, the more you appreciate the beauty of what He is communicating to you and what He is doing in your life.

If you see the Bible as God's loving interaction with you, awesome! Share that eager interaction with others. If you see the Bible as a book of moderately useful, impersonal information you'll miss out on God's transformative truths. Truths that fight the lies surrounding you. Don't miss the opportunity to root yourself in confident hope and meaning. See, the Bible is a compilation of 66 books, written by 40 different authors, used by God to show His relentless love for you and the world.

When you begin to grasp this reality, you can open up the Bible with anticipation and excitement. You will read with a desire to hear what God is saying about Himself and about you, with a willingness to allow Him to change your life!

Why Read?

The main reason to read the Bible is because of what it is—God's primary form of communication to you. STOP. Did you really hear that statement? The Bible is God's primary way of communicating with you. The God of the universe wants to dialogue with you. The God who is infinitely more than you can imagine speaks to you through the Bible! That's amazing. If that was the only reason to read the Bible, it would be all you need, but by God's grace, there is more—reading the Bible benefits you immensely too.

As you learn about God through His Word, He shows you how He designed things to be. The Bible gives you directives on how to love God, how to interact with Him, and how to interact with the world. The Bible also encourages you with stories of people who were changed by God, even in the midst of persecution and pain. The Bible reminds you that the ability to become more like Christ comes from the Holy Spirit, and with the Holy Spirit, you will be able to do great things in Jesus' name. In short, reading the Bible is key to spiritual growth and spiritual effectiveness. The Bible points you to the truth

> *The God who is infinitely more than you can imagine speaks to you through the Bible!*

that both changes your perspective on reality and transforms your life to look more like the loving, truth-speaking, and gracious Jesus. As you read the Bible, you get to know God better, and allow Him to shape your heart and actions to be more of who you are created to be. There are many ways to develop your relationship with God, but the principal way is through reading, studying, reflecting, and inputting God's Word into your life.

The Bible also helps you discern the truth from lies. David states, "Your word is a lamp to guide my feet and a light for my path" (Ps 119:105), and Timothy says, "All Scripture is inspired by God and is useful to teach you what is true and to make you realize what is wrong in your life. It corrects you when you are wrong and teaches you to do what is right. God uses it to prepare and equip his people to do every good work" (2 Tim. 3:16-17). Bible reading is an absolutely crucial practice in your choice to follow Jesus. The Bible is the anchor to your relationship with God and the lighthouse that guides you in how to live. Yes, there are other ways God will guide you, but those are contemplated in the context of what God's Word says. As you read the Bible with this understanding, your reading should transition from a burdensome task to a beautiful discovery of God's relentless love for His people and you. God will expose areas of your life that need to be corrected with a calling to be who He created you to be. You will also find hope; hope because the chaos of this world is not all there is; hope because the pain in this world will one day be redeemed; hope because you have a purpose, and hope because death is not the end.

So, as you read the Bible, read in a way that honors the God. Consume it with appreciation. Understand that God has provided this Word for you out of love, through pain and suffering, so that you can know Him and know hope.

Perhaps your relationship with God is stagnant. Maybe you see other Christians and wish you had a life and faith like them. Wherever you are on your faith journey, I want to encourage you to spend regular time in God's Word. By the Holy Spirit's power, God's Word will transform your relationship with Him, your character, and your interaction in the world. Realize you may not be able to be exactly like another Christian who has been walking in their faith longer than you. It will take time, but you will get there as your faith matures and your experiential knowledge of God grows.

> *By the Holy Spirit's power, God's Word will transform your relationship with Him, your character, and your interaction in the world.*

Why We Don't Read

Before we go any further, we need to address the reasons we don't make reading God's Word a regular part of our life. I share these reasons so you can have your radar tuned to the excuses that draw you away from such a crucial discipline. The reality is there is a massive disconnect between the stated value of Bible reading and the applied value. Ask the majority of Christians if it is important to read the Bible regularly, and you will get a resounding "yes." Yet, if you followed up with the question, "Are you regularly reading the Bible?" you'll find that most of the people who just agreed with the importance will respond with a "no."

A study by *Lifeway Research* revealed this disconnect.

"Forty percent of Americans say the Bible is a book to read over and over again, and yet only 20 percent of Americans say they actually have read all the Bible at least once. Only 22 percent of Americans are systematically, day by day, reading through sections of the Bible." [1]

There are many reasons people don't read the Bible, but the top reasons I've heard are:

1. The Bible is confusing.

2. The Bible is boring and seems out of touch with today.

3. I don't have time (The most common answer).

Perhaps you've been influenced by one of these excuses. You agree that Bible reading is essential, and yet one of these (or all) keeps you from actually diving into God's Word. The good news is that there are relatively easy steps you can take to eliminate these barriers. The bad news is that these "reasons" are often rationalizations that reveal the Bible isn't as important as you say.

For example, the Bible is definitely confusing in places and boring in other places. Still, there are resources to make those verses less confusing and even make some of the very boring parts of the Bible more exciting. (Admittedly, some segments of the Bible are always going to be challenging to read.) My point is: there are tools available that make the confusion understandable and the dullness intriguing. This leads to the question: If there is a way to reduce the confusion and intriguingly understand the Bible, and it's "important," why don't we take the time to invest in these resources? Unfortunately, this is where "I don't have time" becomes the primary excuse. But none of us is as busy as we say we are.

Before you start making a case for how busy you are, let me say it a different way and explain a little before you get angry or even start feeling guilty. There are hours in almost every day where you have time to engage in God's Word. Maybe it's during a fifteen-minute break at work. Maybe it's ten minutes before bedtime. Maybe it's waking up thirty minutes early. Maybe it's eliminating one primetime show a night. Maybe it's telling your kid that they can't be involved in two sports, which have you rushing around each evening in frantic chaos. Maybe it's giving up an evening relaxing at home and joining a bible study. Maybe it's turning the radio off on the drive to work and listening to the Bible. Maybe it's _____.

You get the point: An absence of regular time in God's Word reveals a low value of what the Bible is, and, ultimately, who God is. This may sound harsh, but what valuable relationships are you in which you never talk to one another? Let me guess...none. A growing, vibrant, healthy relationship takes the input of time together.

If you've heard all this and feel pressured to get in gear with God by guilt, let me warn you: being motivated by guilt won't get you very far. If what I just wrote guilts you to action, your outlook is starting on the wrong foundation.

> *An absence of regular time in God's Word reveals a low value of what the Bible is, and, ultimately, who God is.*

Instead, I hope you see that the most powerful, loving, creative, intriguing, and awesome person ever–GOD–wants to have a relationship with you. I pray you will know that God desires to speak His love to you, through His written Word. I also hope you realize that the Bible is one of God's main tools to help you see things properly. To see His love, His redemption, His saving grace, His pursuit of making things right, His good life for you.

See, the Bible provides us a lens to look through to see the unfathomable value of a relationship with God and the glory of a life with Him. Perhaps you've missed the value of God's Word in your life because you're trying to find beauty by looking at the lens instead of using the lens to see God

Discipline

One key thing to remember as you read: Bible reading is a discipline. I'm not talking about punishments, "time outs" or "grounding," but the training of oneself to do something in a habitual and controlled way. In this case, a commitment to read the Bible no matter how tough it may be.

> *Perhaps you've missed the value of God's Word in your life because you're trying to find beauty by looking at the lens instead of using the lens to see God.*

Sometimes people believe those who wake up early to spend time in the Word or take a day away to read and pray are spiritual gurus who love to read, love solitude, and love silent reflection. I think there are some, very few, unique individuals who fit this assumption... BUT I think they are the exception!

Most people who practice consistent time in God's Word do so because they see the value in it, not because it comes easy to them. (As I said before: It's not going to be easy, but it's worth it.) The discipline of consistently inputting God's Word into your life will allow Him to slowly transform you. If you have an expectation that Bible study should be an easy, thrilling adventure, you may be disappointed. But if you discipline yourself, committing to the value of taking in God's Word, you will begin to see that the benefits of regular time in God's Word notably outweigh the difficulty of the discipline.

Study

"Study this Book of Instruction continually. Meditate on it day and night so you will be sure to obey everything written in it. Only then will you prosper and succeed in all you do." (Jos. 1:8)

Study is the discipline of engaging our minds in the things of God for Him to transform us. Like studying a subject in school, this discipline allows us to become more familiar, understand, and grow in interacting with the subject. Romans 12:2 says, "Be transformed by the renewing of your mind" (NIV) Many in our culture accuse Christianity of being a mindless engagement to help us feel better about ourselves, but a mindless approach to our belief is in stark contrast to what we are called to do as Christians. Jesus says, "You will know the truth and the truth will set you free." (Jn. 8:32)

"Know the truth." In other words, there is a mental discipline, a mental exercise that goes into following Jesus. God wants us—all of us—believers and unbelievers to seek the truth, because if you are seeking truth, you will find Truth—God is the creator, and Jesus, His Son, died and rose again for your sins. In knowing THE TRUTH, there is a promise, "the truth will set you free." Jesus invites you to a life of freedom by receiving the gift of His sacrifice for your sins. Accepting the truth of who Jesus is and what He accomplished admits, "Jesus, you know what is best for my life, so teach me how to live a "set free" life."

Naturally, the next step is LISTENING. As I've said before, God communicates with us in many ways, but His key form of communication, of talking with you, is the Bible. His Word shows you what is true, and by studying this truth, you learn how to live out His purpose for your life. This is freedom. Freedom to be what you were created to be, with the love of God who made you with purpose, for a purpose. Studying scripture is a primary discipline because it builds up your understanding of who God is, who you are, and how

God calls you to live. Study has always been central to a life with Christ. This isn't because "a Christian is studious," but because if you love Jesus, you should desire to learn about Him and know Him.

<u>Questions For Reflection:</u>

- Are you reading the Bible regularly? Why or why not?

- For most, the default reading approach is "informational." Is that true for you?

- How might you intentionally approach God's Word in a more "transformational" way?

- If you are regularly studying God's Word, what was it that spurred on that discipline?

- If you aren't, which of the three reasons given define you? (confusing, boring, time) Or is there another one?

- Who is someone you know who regularly reads the Bible, and what can you glean from them to develop a better, more consistent engagement with God's Word?

Chapter 2

The Right Approach Makes
All The Difference

A woman without her man is nothing.

Read that sentence again. How does it set with you? What if I told you your frustration is completely unfounded and based on your flawed interpretation? What if I told you the sentence actually has the exact opposite meaning of what you read? Read twice more, but this time pause where I put the commas.

A woman, without her man is nothing.

A woman without her man, is nothing.

Do you see the differences? One is saying that man is nothing without his woman, and one is saying a woman is nothing without her man. If I had just left the sentence alone, not walking you through the different ways of reading this sentence, you would have been quite confused if I expanded on the sentence in a way that was opposite of your understanding. The good news is there are many tools you can apply to your Bible reading to prevent this type of confusion. This is why proper hermeneutics is so vital to how you engage in God's Word.

Hermeneutics...How To Study

According to Alyssa Roat of Christianity.com, Biblical hermeneutics is "the science of interpretation of the Bible and the methods of that interpretation." [1] The goal of hermeneutics is to correctly interpret and apply what the Bible says. Proper hermeneutics uses methods to prevent incorrect interpretations that come from assumptions readers bring to the text. These methods enhance your reading by drawing you to what the author was trying to communicate in their context. The following overview will give you the tools to eliminate opportunities of confusion, see the beauty of the overarching Biblical narrative, and help you accurately interpret what God is saying to you.

Different Types Of Study

Breadth Study

Breadth study focuses on larger chunks of scripture. In the course of a sitting, you may read multiple chapters or even a single book. This way of studying is excellent for understanding context, the intent of writing, and overarching ideas. A breadth study tends to start with a focus on head knowledge as you gain a general sense of what scripture is addressing. Your broader understanding of the Bible should eventually lead to real-life transformation as you begin to notice larger themes and detailed meanings that can have very personal application.

Breadth study also can be topical. In a topical breadth study, you use resources to find all the scripture references that deal with a certain topic. This type of study can help you understand what the Bible says about the subject as a whole. When doing a topical study, always read the verses in context. Make sure you know what the author is actually saying before assuming an application. (More about this in the AIM section)

Depth Study

Depth study focuses on a smaller group of verses and explores the fullness of their meaning. It looks to see how a particular, smaller set of verses is being used to instruct, guide, reprove, praise, etc. Like breadth study, depth studies need to understand the surrounding verses and chapters to make sure the interpretation is congruent with the author's overall purpose. Depth study mulls over a small passage, again and again, to let it sink deep in your soul. A depth study usually involves commentaries and other resources to find out as much as you can about the subject/ verses.

Exegesis (ek-suh-jee-suhs) vs. Eisegesis (I-sah-jee-suhs)

Here are two fancy words that have significant implications on how you read the Bible correctly. Eisegesis occurs when you read and interpret the Bible with your own agendas, presuppositions, and biases. Basically, eisegesis is the reader imposing his or her interpretation into the text without proper Bible study. A simple way to remember "eisegesis," which is pronounced "I-sah-jee-suhs." is; "eisegesis is when I read my thoughts and opinions into the verses," or "I put my meaning into the verse." Eisegesis is a common mistake and should be avoided because, out of context, you can make the Bible say pretty much whatever "I" want.

Take, for example, a familiar verse that is incorrectly eisegeted: "For I know the plans I have for you," says the Lord. "They are plans for good and not for disaster, to give you a future and a hope" (Jer. 29:11). This is a favorite verse for Christians to use to show that God will bless them and guide them; it's kind of a spiritual security blanket. While I believe that God does have a plan and wants to bless His people, the context of this verse is often missed for the sake of the reader's own desire to "feel good about God and life." Eisegesis says, "This verse is for me, and it's God's promise to make my life work out for the good of worldly blessings and comfort."

Well, this eisegetical interpretation is just wrong. Again, not that God doesn't have a plan for your life, but this verse wasn't written to you and does not promise that a life with Jesus is all rainbows and lollipops. Nor is it a promise that if you just have more robust faith, life will get better, and you'll cheerfully see all the bad things in your life are actually really good. Reading the Bible eisegetically may look like googling "God's promises," which highlights several verses without context, inviting you to a poor understanding of God's actual promises to you. This methodology can leave you discouraged and disenfranchised when those promises aren't what you incorrectly assumed.

A proper reading of Jeremiah 29:11 will show you this verse (and the whole book of Jeremiah) is in the context of a harsh rebuke to the people of Israel who are in exile because they disobeyed God. They are far from home and in despair because God has used a pagan nation to overtake them. If you go back just one verse, you will read, "You will be in Babylon for seventy years. But then I will come and do for you all the good things I have promised, and I will bring you home again" (Jer. 29:10). So, the result of this promise wasn't an immediate change in positivity, with Israel returning home to live happily ever after. Life was still extremely difficult for a long time, and I can guarantee that many Israelites died before God fulfilled this promise. This often quoted, pump you up, "it's all gonna work out for your good," is a promise to Israel who still experienced another seventy years of torment.

As you can see in this example, many people place their ideas into the verse. They read it out of context to get what they want and miss what is truly being said. I don't share this to discourage you but to help you realize that a proper way of reading the Bible grants you an ability to better interpret what is being communicated. Eisegesis may have partial truth in it, so don't discredit it completely. Instead, let it be a warning to tread carefully and practice the correct hermeneutic.

Exegesis (ex-ah-jee-suhs) is the opposite of eisegesis. It is the proper way of approaching your reading because it will give you a more accurate, profound, and beautiful picture of what God is saying. "Exegesis" exhumes or explores the infor-

> *Exegesis is the proper way of approaching your reading because it will give you a more accurate, profound, and beautiful picture of what God is saying.*

mation from the text. Exegesis gathers the meaning from the text rather than reading meaning into the text. Sometimes you will need to use outside sources to gain a better understanding (cultural, literary, and historical), but, at a minimum, exegesis is always aware of the written context. Later in this chapter, I'll give you more tools to help you correctly exegete your reading. The example and conclusion of Jeremiah 29:11 in the previous paragraph provides a beginning idea of how to exegete a verse.

God's Word Trumps Our Culture's Perspective

When you see the Bible as God's Word to you, you must also hold firm that God's Word trumps our personal and cultural perspectives. Jesus claims to be "the Truth," and with much prayer, scrutiny, and diligent discussion, the church's history has held to the belief that the Bible is God's Word of Truth to us. The direct implications of Jesus' claim of 'Truth' and the claim that the Bible is God's Word of Truth are this: if culture opposes God's Word, either God's Word is untrue, or the culture's belief is untrue. The belief that the Bible is God's Word settles that argument, and God's Word wins. This does not mean that the Bible is without tensions. It does mean that you need to study those tensions responsibly, giving the benefit of the doubt to God's Word, not to the current and ever-changing, underdeveloped, cultural perspective.

> *If culture opposes God's Word, either God's Word is untrue, or the culture's belief is untrue.*

These are the starting blocks for correctly interpreting the Bible, but there are many more resources which will significantly enhance your reading, steering you away from misinterpreting scripture. Remember, your approach to God's Word considerably impacts the transformative effect it should have on your life.

Questions For Reflection:

- In which of the two types of study (Breadth and Depth) do you most often participate?

- What would it mean for your life if each time you studied God's Word, you allowed it to shape your actions and attitudes?

- What areas of your life have you not allowed God's Word to transform?

- Do you understand the difference between eisegesis and exegesis? If so, write down, in your own words, the difference. If you have any questions for clarification, write those down and seek out someone to answer them.

- "God's Word trumps the culture's perspective." This includes your own bias and how you think things should be. Are there any areas of your life where you are making excuses not to align with what God's Word says? Explain

Chapter 3

Context Is Key

My Dad took my brothers and me to a charity hockey game when I was in middle school, and the excitement on the ice concluded with a live auction in the stands. My twin brother and I decided to run around the top of the bleachers since we didn't have any money and needed to work off some energy after sitting through the game. Dad remained lower in the stands, and as the auctioneer began calling out items, we took our cue to sit still until the bidding was over. A few items which I wasn't interested in were auctioned off. Then a signed stick by one of my favorite players was placed on the stage.

The bidding started, and hands started raising to offer the next highest bid. I was about ten rows up from my Dad and was eager to get his attention to see if he would make a bid for "us." Intent on using telepathy to get his attention, I thought hard, "Dad, look this way!" Whenever he moved, twisted, or gave any sign that my mental powers were getting through to him, I waved my hand to continue beckoning his attention. A few times I thought I had him, I thought he'd turn, but no luck.

After a few attempts, I noticed one of the guys down the row glaring at me as he made yet another bid. Confused at his hostile attitude toward me, I tried one more time to wave my Dad's attention toward me. My hand went up, and for the first time, I heard, "$200 to the young man in the back." Wait, what? The auctioneer was pointing at me. I didn't have $200. He completely misinterpreted what I was doing. I was just raising my hand and waving...like everyone who was bidding!!! OH, NO! Fear overwhelmed me because I was the one who was wrong. I was not interpreting the context of the room. I was going to be on the hook for all that money. I looked over to the man down the row, who was still glaring, and like an angel from heaven, he begrudgingly raised his hand to claim his prize. (I have no idea how long I was in an unknown bidding war).

If I were to ask you, "What do you call it when someone elevates their arm over their head and shakes their hand back and forth?" You'd probably say "waving." If I gave you the same description in the context of a charity auction, your answer, your interpretation of that action, would correctly change to "bidding for an item."

It's the same with the Bible. Context is key to understanding what is happening and what God has called us to do. Without knowledge of the context, we can easily miss the point, be appalled by what we are reading, or worst of all, abandon our faith to "a bunch of crazy fairytales" and "unfulfilled promises."

Literary Context

One of the main ways you can avoid the mistake of taking things in the Bible out of context is by reading large sections of the Bible at a time. This is called 'literary context.' It's great that you have your favorite Bible verses, but to avoid misusing or missing the rich depth of a verse, they need to be read within a broader literary context. Here are a few examples of the dangers of reading verses out of context, as well as the enriching reality that each verse points to within its correct context.

Romans 8:28 states, "And we know that God causes everything to work together for the good of those who love God and are called according to his purpose for them." This is a great verse that offers genuine hope, but out of context, many people assume that it is a Biblical promise that if you love God, everything will work out okay. As you know (or will know), life often doesn't "work out" the way you think, and doesn't for the millions of Christians who have been killed, starved to death, died of cancer, drowned, gone bankrupt, been divorced, and the list could go on.

Suppose you read this verse as a promise for a "good life" and things go terribly wrong. In that case, you are left with three options:

1. Accuse yourself of not really loving God.

2. Accuse God of lying.

3. Dismiss the reality of this promise.

These conclusions are dangerous and can be avoided by simply reading the verse within the context of the surrounding chapters and books. I challenge you to do so, because you will see that Paul is writing to people suffering for their faith. He is not offering them a car salesman talk of "put a smile on…it's all going to work out for you just fine."

Instead, this verse is an encouragement to hold on to hope that God's plan is good, and whatever you face in this life, God will work it out for a grander, glorifying story. This is also an encouragement, when persecuted, to remember there is an amazing eternity beyond this life and to be reminded that you have God's Spirit with you now.

These words are written amid persecution and weakness, and Paul offers a reminder of hope because in the end, there will be a "happily ever after" if you follow Christ... It will all work out (though the promise may not be fulfilled in this life). The surrounding verses, with no extra resources, help reveal the truth of what is being said. There is a big difference between reading these verses as an affirmation of our American dream and seeing them in the correct context: As an encouragement that life may be full of pain, but Jesus wins. One is about you and your plans. The other is about God and His fulfilled plan.

Here is another example of the importance of literary context. One of the most well-known Bible verses is John 3:16, "For this is how God loved the world: He gave His one and only Son so that everyone who believes in him will not perish but have eternal life." By itself, it's a great sentence to memorize, but don't stop there. By looking at the surrounding verses, you will see an even richer revelation of what God is communicating. Just adding the next verse deepens your understanding, "God sent his Son into the world not to judge the world, but to save the world through him" (3:17).

But don't stop there; go a little further, and these loving, joy-focused verses hold with them a warning to those who reject Jesus and a calling to those who accept His gift. The verses continue; "There is no judgment against anyone who believes in him. But anyone who does not believe in him has already been judged for not believing in God's one and only Son. And the judgment is based on this fact: God's light came into the world, but people loved the darkness more than the light, for their actions were evil. All who do evil hate the light and refuse to go near it for fear their sins will be exposed. But those who do what is right come to the light so others can see that they are doing what God wants" (3:18-21).

Does God love the world so much that He gave us Jesus? Yes. But the context tells a fuller story. It's only through Jesus that we are saved. There will be judgment for those who reject Him. Those who accept Jesus are able to live lives obedient to God, in order to show others God's love.

As we've seen with these examples, when we take verses out of context there is a great danger of the scripture being misused or under-realized. Implementing good hermeneutics and using exegesis rather

> *When we take verses out of context there is a great danger of the scripture being misused or under-realized.*

than eisegesis will enhance your reading and save you from some of these pitfalls. Here are more tools to help the exegesis process.

Historical Context

The next step in properly interpreting God's Word takes a bit more time and will need extra-biblical tools. Study Bibles, commentaries, and other books can provide information about each book's historical setting that will deeply enrich your understanding. There are excellent resources online that provide the historical context of each book of the Bible. While these take more investment of your time, the value of learning about the historical context can better illuminate the beauty and significance of what God is communicating through the writers.

Here is an example of a Bible story that disturbs many people when they first read it… because it is read without historical context.

"Abraham!" God called.

"Yes," he replied. "Here I am."

"Take your son, your only son—yes, Isaac, whom you love so much—and go to the land of Moriah. Go and sacrifice him as a burnt offering on one of the mountains, which I will show you."

The next morning Abraham got up early. He saddled his donkey and took two of his servants with him, along with his son, Isaac. Then he chopped wood for a fire for a burnt offering and set out for the place God had told him about. On the third day of their journey, Abraham looked up and saw the place in the distance. "Stay here with the donkey," Abraham told the servants. "The boy and I will travel a little farther. We will worship there, and then we will come right back."

So Abraham placed the wood for the burnt offering on Isaac's shoulders, while he himself carried the fire and the knife. As the two of them walked on together, Isaac turned to Abraham and said, "Father?"

"Yes, my son?" Abraham replied.

"We have the fire and the wood," the boy said, "but where is the sheep for the burnt offering?"

"God will provide a sheep for the burnt offering, my son," Abraham answered. And they both walked on together.

When they arrived at the place where God had told him to go, Abraham built an altar and arranged the wood on it. Then he tied his son, Isaac, and laid him on the altar on top of the wood. And Abraham picked up the knife to kill his son as a sacrifice. At that moment the angel of the Lord called to him from heaven, "Abraham! Abraham!"

"Yes," Abraham replied. "Here I am!"

"Don't lay a hand on the boy!" the angel said. "Do not hurt him in any way, for now I know that you truly fear God. You have not withheld from me even your son, your only son."

Then Abraham looked up and saw a ram caught by its horns in a thicket. So he took the ram and sacrificed it as a burnt offering in place of his son" (Gen. 22:1-13).

Reading this story without context would probably lead you to think, "What kind of God is this? That's just sick. A loving God wouldn't do that." Unfortunately, many people dismiss these thoughts because the "end justifies the means," or they accuse a perfect, loving God of being neither perfect nor loving. Both of these miss the mark.

Instead, there is a third way that involves looking at the historical context of this story, and, when seen in that context, the 'means' makes more sense. Incredibly, when understanding the context, the account becomes an affirmation of God's love. Let's look at the historical context and see how that happens.

Abraham is from the land of Ur. This is a land devoted to worshipping false gods in really disturbing ways, one of which is child sacrifice. Genesis, the book that records this account, is written to the people of Israel who are surrounded by nations and people groups who practice child sacrifice. In Abraham's context, and the context in which the Israelites lived, it wasn't abnormal to hear stories of child sacrifices to the gods. So, when Abraham is told to sacrifice his son, it's not some wildly forceful arm-twisting God that menacingly uses to get Abraham to obey. It's a normal request. Does that make it less disturbing? No, but the story isn't over. We need to continue our work and pair the historical context with the surrounding literary context.

Once again, this story is often incorrectly read as primarily focusing on Abraham's obedience. Abraham's obedience is impressive and should be praised, but the context (both historical and literary) of this story shows the reader that the primary reason for this story is not Abraham's obedience. This story's focus is revealed when God stops Abraham from following through with the sacrifice and provides a ram to be sacrificed instead. So, the ends justify the means? No, and yes. No, in the context we often read. Yes, in its correct context. Here is what I mean:

Instead of a sadistic God who is trying to see how far He can push people to obedience, the story shows God's faithfulness and God's love in OPPOSITION to the surrounding gods' requirements. In other words, God is saying, "I am not like those other gods. I'm setting myself apart from them as distinctly different. You thought I was like those other gods, but I want to make it clear that I am not. I am faithful to my promise and my love for you. Unlike those gods, I will not make you sacrifice your son."

Now, wait for it... As we read the story in the broader Biblical context, we also see that God's provision of a ram is an allusion to Jesus. In place of Abraham's son, the ram God provides is a statement from God that "A sacrifice is still needed for sin... but...I will provide a sacrifice for you." The ultimate, God-provided sacrifice is Jesus!

Yes, thousands of years before Jesus, God was setting the stage to let people know He is righteous and merciful, and Jesus is the sacrifice we need. God interacted with Abraham in this way to show that we can't provide what is necessary for our own justification, but that God can, and will, (and now has) through Jesus. WOW!!!!!

Knowing the historical and literary context changes this once disturbing account to a stunning statement of God's faithfulness and love, distinguishing Himself from all other gods. The historical and literary context reveals the story isn't primarily about obedience. It's primarily about God's love and faithfulness. Context changes it from an odd account at the beginning of the Bible to one pointing to the entire redemptive plan of God through Jesus. Context is key.

Cultural Context

There's one more thing to remember when you read the Bible in context. The historical and cultural context of each book of the Bible was considerably different than today. You may think that's a "duh" statement, but the implications are important in how you interact with God's Word. If you read the Bible, critiquing it to your current cultural view, you may interpret things that the author never meant. Approaching the Bible, assuming your cultural context into the text (eisegesis), can lead to conclusions that were never part of the discourse.

Here's an example: We live in a time where the role of women is seen as equal to men (whether or not there is equality that way, I am not here to argue). The point is this. It is generally assumed, in our culture, that all jobs can be done by either men or women. This has not always been the case. Only a few decades

> *Approaching the Bible, assuming your cultural context into the text, can lead to conclusions that were never part of the discourse.*

ago, the culture held a perspective that there were jobs which only men could do. Again, I'm not saying that was right or wrong, but if you were to ask the culture 50, 60, or 1000 years ago, if there were jobs that only men could do, most everyone would say "yes." Even bringing it up for discussion would probably be confusing because it was a culturally held assumption (by both men and women).

In the same way, we can read things in the Bible, which we may want to question, while the original readers wouldn't even think to ask. An example of this is the Bible's lack of direct condemnation of slavery. A lot of people have used the Bible's silence on slavery (and even what seems like the promotion of slavery) to question the loving morality of God. This is where understanding the historical and cultural context can help move us beyond our own cultural assumptions.

First, many people assume that the slavery that the Bible appears to be okay with is the same type of slavery we see in American history. In fact, the slavery mentioned in the Bible is vastly different than our cultural context of slavery. *The Lexham Bible Dictionary* states slavery in ancient times is, "The practice of one person owning another as property, or one person owing a debt to another and repaying that debt via their labor. Found in the ancient Near East, the Greco-Roman world, and the Old and New Testaments. No single description of slavery fits the various forms it took in the ancient world. However, it was quite different from the slavery practiced in the West during the 18th and 19th centuries." [1]

This means that our cultural understanding of slavery is not the same as the Biblical usage of the term "slave." Slavery, in Israel's context, was an agreed-upon "work for debt" program. On top of that, God established the Year of Jubilee, which occurred every 50 years to wipe away all debt and allow slaves to return to their family's land. "In addition, you must count off seven Sabbath years, seven sets of seven years, adding up to forty-nine years in all. Then on the Day of Atonement in the fiftieth year, blow the ram's horn loud and long throughout the land. Set this year apart as holy, a time to proclaim freedom throughout the land for all who live there. It will be a jubilee year for you, when each of you may return to the land that belonged to your ancestors and return to your own clan" (Lev. 25:8-10).

Second, when slavery is viewed under the whole Biblical narrative, it's clear that the Bible speaks against treating any humans the way slaves were treated in American history. The idea of freedom and equality is expanded upon in the New Testament where Paul says, "There is no longer Jew or Gentile, slave or free, male and female. For you are all one in Christ Jesus" (Gal. 3:28). In Paul's culture slavery did exist, but he redefines relational status between all believers. Through Christ's work, our hearts are to embrace relational equality. In another of His letters, Paul writes to his friend Philemon, whose slave (Onesimus) has run away. In the letter, Paul states his reason for writing: "that you might have him (Onesimus) back forever—no longer as a slave, but better than a slave, as a dear brother. He is very dear to me but even dearer to you, both as a fellow man and as a brother in the Lord" (Philem. 1:16, NIV). This is just another example that reminds us to not read the Bible with our twenty-first century cultural assumptions. Context is key.

Questions For Reflection:

- What are some Bible verses you know or have heard…go back to those and read the surrounding verses or chapter and reflect on the expanded contextual understanding of the verse. How has the verse gained meaning? How might it have lost some of the meaning you thought it had? How does the literary context help you use the verse properly?

- Historical context is often not found in the literary context since the authors were writing to the people of that time, so how might you gain a better understanding of historical context? (hint: see chapter 6)

- C.S. Lewis used the term "chronological snobbery" to describe "the assumption that whatever is new is true with an uncritical acceptance of the most current thought."[2] Truth isn't to be assumed just because an idea is new. If that were the case, we could have no confidence in what we now believe because the future will be new and supplant our current truth. Instead, we must evaluate things based on their inherent claims. Not based on newness or the current cultural assumptions. How might your twenty-first-century mindset incorrectly influence your interpretation of the Bible? What areas of the Bible make you uncomfortable because they are in tension with our current social climate?

Chapter 4

Seeing Jesus Everywhere

If the context is key, you might ask any of these questions.

"What about the claims that the Old Testament has hundreds of foreshadowing verses of Jesus?"

"If the authors of the Old Testament books didn't know about Jesus, how can we come to a conclusion that the Old Testament was revealing something they were unaware of?"

"If Jesus wasn't known to the Old Testament authors, isn't that 'Eisgetically' reading Him into the story?"

Great questions! Seeing Jesus in everything is a bit divergent from strict adherence to context. Still, you are afforded that ability for three reasons.

1. Even though the Bible is made up of many different authors who had limited knowledge and perspective, God, who has full

knowledge and perspective, was guiding each author's writings. God used each author to communicate with specific people in their time, using the writer's gifts, understanding, and passions. At the same time, God mysteriously guides each book's crafting to communicate beyond the immediate context. The Old Testament has many verses which seem to be obviously about Jesus. Most of these verses have a double meaning—one being what the author meant in his immediate context, and one in which God is telling a grander story. In the book of Isaiah, some verses that are read as prophetic statements about Jesus are, in their initial context, about the Persian King Cyrus, yet they are entirely realized in Jesus, the ultimate King who completely fulfills the prophecies.

2. In 2 Corinthians 3, Paul says, "Since this new way gives us such confidence, we can be very bold. We are not like Moses, who put a veil over his face so the people of Israel would not see the glory, even though it was destined to fade away. But the people's minds were hardened, and to this day whenever the old covenant is being read, the same veil covers their minds so they cannot understand the truth. And this veil can be removed only by believing in Christ. Yes, even today when they read Moses' writings, their hearts are covered with that veil, and they do not understand. But whenever someone turns to the Lord, the veil is taken away." (vv. 12-16)

The "veil" is being blind to spiritual realities and truth. When we give our lives to Jesus, it changes everything, redefines everything, and we can see Jesus more clearly, without a "veil." When we believe in Jesus, the Holy Spirit indwells us, opening our eyes to see how God is communicating at a whole different level through His Word, through all time, in all of creation.

3. The first chapter in John explains something profound to our understanding of Jesus, which has a direct implication on how we read His Word.

"In the beginning the Word already existed. The Word was with God, and the Word was God. He existed in the beginning with God. (vv.1-2)

"The Word" refers to Jesus and is clarified in verse 14; "So the Word became human and made his home among us. He was full of unfailing love and faithfulness. And we have seen his glory, the glory of the Father's one and only Son." Pastor John Piper says, "John calls Jesus the Word because he (John) had come to see the words of Jesus as the truth of God and the person of Jesus as the truth of God in such a unified way that Jesus himself—in his coming, and working, and teaching, and dying and rising—was the final and decisive message of God. Or to put it more simply: what God had to say to us was not only or mainly what Jesus said, but who Jesus was and what he did."[1]

So, if Jesus is the Word, and Jesus is God, and Jesus is who and what God says, then his entire Word (the Bible) would have echoes of Jesus everywhere. On top of that, Jesus quotes the Old Testament, revealing what the original authors and readers may not have known...This all points to Him.

> *If Jesus is the Word, and Jesus is God, and Jesus is who and what God says, then his entire Word (the Bible) would have echoes of Jesus everywhere.*

When you read the Bible as God's Word, revealing Jesus throughout, you will see truths more profoundly, read stories with grander understanding, and see the whole Bible as a story that leads us to Him.

<u>Questions For Reflection:</u>

- Have you ever read the Old Testament with a perspective of finding foreshadowing of Jesus? If so, how did that impact your reading? If not, how does this approach change your perspective of the Old Testament?

- Read Exodus 12 and 1 Peter 1:17-25: How is the Exodus story a foreshadowing of Christ?

- Read 2 Samuel 7:11b-17 (Samuel is referring to Solomon throughout this quote) and Luke 1:26-22. How is Solomon's life and reign a foreshadowing of Christ? (hint: Luke 11:31)

Chapter 5

A.I.M. And Other Tools

"I cannot believe CANNOT BELIEVE he said that!" A conversation I walked into included shocking words that hurt me deeply. I spent the next few weeks steaming about what my friend had said and the fact that it seemed like no big deal to him at all. I shared what was said with a handful of people who were also extremely put off by the words spoken. All the advice I received affirmed my gigantic frustration and pain. In the most gracious way I could, I wrote an email (bad idea) to discuss what he had said. It wasn't long before I read the response to my email, which was clearly filled with anger, hurt, and frustration at my anger, hurt, and frustration.

When we met, the room was thick with tension. Both of us were fuming. The conversation was emotional, and we both shared the pain we experienced from each other. Though the relationship was damaged and took years to heal, I look back on our communication and see the issue catalyzed by how each of us interpreted what the other person said. My friend was very offended that I had interpreted what he said to be so offensive. He was making a joke and was really trying to say something nice about me. On the other hand, he interpreted my email as walking away from any future relationship. The very reason I sent the email was to fight for the relationship. Two well-intentioned communications were terribly misinterpreted by not considering the source, by not asking, "What was my friend actually trying to say?"

A.I.M. — Author's Intended Meaning

To help you exegete verses correctly, ask this one simple question whenever you read: "What's the AIM of this passage?" or "What is the Author's Intended Meaning?" Do not start your reading by asking, "What is the Bible saying to me?" This is because the Bible wasn't first written to you and whatever you have going on in your life could skew your perspective of what is being communicated. When you start by seeking the author's intended

> *The Bible wasn't first written to you and whatever you have going on in your life could skew your perspective of what is being communicated.*

meaning, you avoid the opportunity to eisegete your own thoughts into the Word.

For an example that reveals the importance of "AIM," let's look at the differences between the four Gospels (Matthew, Mark, Luke, John). In his book *The Gospels In Harmony*, Dr. John Barnett states:

"The Gospels record Christ's ministry to the four groups of people then and now in the world. The Jews who loved the Scriptures and the prophecies of God. They would only listen to one of their own. So Matthew speaks to the Jews and the deeply religious of our day. Mark spoke to the Romans. These were the leaders and leadership, and action impressed them. They knew nothing of Scriptures but everything of power. So, to this group comes the action-packed Gospel of the powerful ministry of Christ. Mark uses the word *'and'* 1,375 times to tie together the endless actions of Christ. Like our modern successful business men and women, they want a God who can powerfully meet their deepest needs. Luke was a Greek speaking to the Greeks. The Greeks loved culture, beauty and ideas. Happiness could be found in the pursuit of truth. Luke fills his book with insights, interviews, songs, and details that fascinate the inquiring mind. So today the truth seekers find Jesus in Luke! John wrote to everyone, because everyone needs to meet God and only Jesus can reveal Him. In this book we meet an absolutely powerful God in human flesh who controls and rules the universe He created."[1]

As you can see, there is great value in knowing who the audience is and what the author is trying to accomplish. Not just so you are smarter, but because when you do see the author's intended meaning, it enhances the meaning for you! The other benefits you get from discovering the author's intended meaning is clarity in why one author includes specific details not included by the others, and why each book is nuanced in what is addressed.

The author's intent also has significant implications for how you interpret God's Word for yourself. You'll find the value of asking "What is the author's intended meaning?" from the very first pages of the Bible. The book of Genesis has been highly controversial, especially in modern times. Our culture lives within the age of "scientific enlightenment," a perspective that filters everything through the lens of testable, repeatable science. Genesis is no foreigner to scientific scrutiny. Some of the greatest opponents of Christianity use the Genesis story of creation as their most prominent reason for the "absurdity of the Bible." In this short section, I'm not going to settle the argument, but I want to show you that when the book of Genesis is interpreted through the author's intended meaning, many (not all) of the tensions of scientific opposition to the Bible are relieved.

When you scientifically critique Genesis, you are reading yourself and your 21st century perspective onto the writing (Eisegesis). This approach assumes, "since I exist in a scientific reasoning culture, Genesis must speak the language of science." The problem with this is the author and the audience of Genesis were not asking the same scientific questions you and I may assume are being answered in Genesis. Quantum mechanics, atoms, nuclear reactions, and physics are all things utterly foreign to the author. So, when we look at Genesis as an account intended to answer scientific questions, we are reading it in a way that the author didn't intend.

Let me give you some context that may help clear up some of the confusion. The author (historically assigned to Moses) lived in a culture surrounded by hundreds of different gods who lorded their "god-ness" over humans in impersonal and authoritative ways, often demanding worshippers do abhorrent things. The Biblical story of creation is written to reveal the True God, who is drastically dissimilar from all other false gods. The Bible's account of creation presents a God who brought order out of chaos and created the universe out of love for humans. It shows a God whose intent was to be in a loving, harmonious relationship with His people. Genesis shows a God who gifts creation to humans and invites them to trust Him.

Unfortunately, Genesis also reveals humanity's rejection of God, desiring autonomy over a relationship with Him. The rest of the Bible shares the story of a God who, despite being rejected, continues to pursue a relationship with humanity. See, the author's intended meaning wasn't to answer the question, "How was the world scientifically created?" That's not a question that was even on the radar of the author. The creation story instead is meant to answer, "Who is the true God? Who are we? And what type of god is the True God?" When we explore and understand the author's intended meaning, we see the Bible in the correct light. Our reading becomes so much richer, more accurate, and more beautiful.

A desire to find the author's intended meaning should lead to the next question: "How do I find out the writer's intent?" I've given you a few tools already, and the next few sections will equip you with even more ways to discover the A.I.M. of a passage.

Avoid Individualism

Our modern culture is very individualistic. We think of ourselves as independent beings, separate from culture and society. In contrast, most communities throughout history celebrated and embraced collectivism: a belief that identity and understanding were not found in the individual self but in participating in the context of the larger group.

While each person is an individual, the individual was indivisible from the community of which they were part. The implications of this can be clearly seen in the people of Israel.

Perhaps you've read one of the many stories about Israel's worship of idols and God's punishment of all Israel for this sin. If you're anything like me, you've thought, "Surely not every single person worshipped the idol… and yet God punishes all… that seems unfair." Do you see the

> *Collectivism:*
> *a belief that identity*
> *and understanding were*
> *not found in the individ-*
> *ual self but in participat-*
> *ing in the context*
> *of the larger group.*

cultural assumption of individualism you've brought into your reading? In times like this, you need to set aside your cultural bias of individualism and realize that even if some are not participating in the sin, they are part of the sin because they are part of the group who has turned from God.

Maybe this is helpful. Imagine you kicked your brother (or someone in your family) and broke his rib, and your parents found out and rightly decided to ground you for three months. It would be unreasonable for you to argue that just your foot should be punished, but your hands, eyes, mouth, ears, torso, and other leg should not be punished since they didn't participate in the kicking.

"But that's dumb," you might say. "Of course, all of you would get punished because your foot isn't a separate thing on its own!" Oh, but it is separate—if I showed you a picture of an ear and a foot and asked if these two things are different, by function, appearance, and brain interaction, you should say, "yes." Do they belong to one body and is the whole body held responsible? "Yes." Although your individualistic perspective fights against this analogy (I know because I do), a collective perspective is more in line with how people have thought for most of history.

Again, when reading the Bible, you have to remove yourself from a "just me" thinking and realize you are inextricably tied to others. "Just you" is not "just you." You are part of an "us," whether that is God's people, your family, community, sports team, or work team. In the same way, most books of the Bible are written to communities and need to be read with that perspective. The perspective of community is crucial to Biblical interpretation.

Prescription vs. Description

Another critical question to ask when studying the Bible is, "Are these verses prescriptive or descriptive?" To remember what each of these words means, think:

'Prescriptive' is like a doctor telling you what to do (think: prescription). Prescriptive texts are instructive commands of what to do, what not to do, and they guide you in Christ-like living.

'Descriptive' texts are merely describing what has occurred. Descriptive texts may have applications for you but drawing a direct application from a descriptive text usually has a foundation in other verses or through overarching consistent ethics or narratives.

> *Prescriptive texts are instructive commands of what to do, what not to do, and they guide you in Christ-like living. Descriptive texts are merely describing what has occurred.*

Let's take a look at prescriptive and descriptive verses. Most of Jesus' direct teaching is prescriptive. Jesus, as the authority on life, tells His listeners to repent, love enemies, not murder, not commit adultery, not worry, and much more (see Mt 4-6). These are prescriptive because Jesus is directly telling the listeners how to live. While many of Jesus' teaching are clearly prescriptive, a lot of the confusion between prescriptive or descriptive verses comes when reading the Old Testament books and some of the New Testament parables.

One commonly misinterpreted Old Testament story is the story of David and Goliath. 1 Samuel 17 is a descriptive account of young David trusting God will give him what he needs to take down the giant (which the rest of Israel was terrified to fight). With just a sling and a stone, little David defeats the giant Goliath.

If you were to assume this was a prescriptive story, you could conclude some pretty wild things: I should try to slay anyone taunting God's people. If I face a bully, I should approach him with no fear, knowing God is on my side and will take Him out. As followers of God, we should destroy anyone who opposes Him. While those are seriously misaligned with the text and a bit easier to weed out, you've probably heard some other incorrect prescriptive interpretations—If you face your 'giants,' you'll slay them. If you just have confident faith, God will deliver you from peril. God will use little things to do big things; you just have to pick up the stone.

Does the story of David and Goliath reveal that each of these statements are true? Yes—for David, in that circumstance...but that is not a prescriptive promise for everyone. This story describes a time and person in Israel's history who God used to do great things, not a list of things you can do to assure that any of life's "giants" will be defeated.

Let's move to the New Testament and look at an interaction Jesus has with a rich young ruler to see another example of misreading descriptive Bible verses. Matthew records an interaction Jesus has with a rich young man who asks what he must do to receive eternal life. After telling Jesus about all the laws he has followed Jesus says to him, "If you want to be perfect, go and sell all your possessions and give the money to the poor, and you will have treasure in heaven. Then come, follow me" (Mt. 19:21). Reading these verses as prescriptive would lead you to believe everyone who wants to enter into God's Kingdom HAS TO sell everything they own.

Does this text have implications for your money? Absolutely, but it is not a prescription that anyone who believes in Jesus needs to sell everything they have. On the other hand: Can God call people to sell everything for His Kingdom? Absolutely. Don't make the other mistake of dismissing yourself from what God may call you to do. But don't use this text as a prescription for all believers.

To correctly interpret the story of the "rich young ruler," you need to read the verses in both their immediate context and the broader Biblical context. Once again, starting with the following question will help you understand what is being said: "Is this something Jesus is prescribing for all people or a description of an interaction He had?"

While the interaction with the rich young ruler shows God's desire for our hearts and wallets to be wholly His, this is a descriptive text. You can know this because Jesus doesn't ask every person He encounters to sell everything. The book of Acts tells us that Christians met in houses (their church gatherings), meaning someone didn't sell everything they own. Later on, in the book of First Timothy, Paul writes, "As for the rich in this present age, charge them not to be haughty, nor to set their hopes on the uncertainty of riches, but on God, who richly provides us with everything to enjoy. They are to do good, to be rich in good works, to be generous and ready to share, thus storing up treasure for themselves as a good foundation for the future, so that they may take hold of that which is truly life" (1 Tim. 6:17-19, ESV).

These First Timothy verses are a prescription of proper actions and attitudes the rich should have with their money: Don't put your hope in your riches. Instead, use your riches to do good for God's Kingdom. But notice the assumption with this prescriptive statement: There are rich people...and notice what the prescription doesn't say: "Tell the rich in the world to sell everything they have." On top of this, I believe the reason Matthew shares the conversation with the rich man is to draw the reader to Jesus' response to the question the disciples ask as the rich man walks away dejected. "Who in the world can be saved?" Jesus responds, "Humanly speaking, it is impossible. But with God everything is possible"(Mt. 19:25-26). In other words, "the prescription" is: We must seek God for salvation because it is priceless and there is no amount of good work we can do to earn it.

A couple of questions to help determine whether you're reading prescriptive or descriptive texts are:

- Is the Bible telling me how something should be (prescriptive) or describing something that has happened (descriptive)?

- What is the context of the text I am reading? Is it addressing a unique situation or presenting a principle to live by?

- Are there other texts in the Scriptures that back up the command? If so, then it's probably prescriptive. If not, ask question 2.

Commentary

Have you ever heard a pastor speak about the history and meaning of a passage which had you wishing you could "see that information" in the text? Well, I've got good news: You don't need a pastor to access that information. You need a good commentary. A commentary is a series of notes explaining the meaning, context, author, and ideas presented in the text.

There are many different commentaries. Some are incredibly in-depth and would take time in seminary to understand. Others are written in ways middle schoolers would quickly benefit from. Commentaries are not just something for pastors—they are helpful to all Bible readers. Although it may seem daunting, reading a commentary will be hugely beneficial to your correct comprehension. It will also enlighten your reading in insightful ways. Most of what we have discussed regarding knowing the genre, reading in context, understanding the AIM,

> *A commentary is a series of notes explaining the meaning, context, author, and ideas presented in the text.*

and navigating whether texts are prescriptive or descriptive, can be found in a good commentary. The first level of 'commentary' is a study Bible. This type of Bible will have book introductions as well as footnotes throughout your reading which give brief explanations of chapters and verses. For a much more thorough resource, I highly recommend Dr. Tom Constable's commentary, which is FREE online at www.soniclight.com. Dr. Constable's commentary is a relatively easy resource on all the books of the Bible, with an introduction to each book that includes the date of writing, author, scope, purpose, theology, structure, outline, message, as well as a verse-by-verse walk-through of what is written. It's incredible.

As with Bible reading, it is helpful to have someone to talk with about what you've read in the commentary. A commentary may not answer all your questions, but it will provide profound insight from people who have studied the original languages, history, and meaning. As a warning, there are some bad commentaries, and others may be really hard to understand, so be sure to ask trusted people for suggestions. Commentaries are a great resource that can give you a fuller picture of what God might be saying through the text.

The Bible Project

Another great resource is www.thebibleproject.com. This website has access to short, animated video overviews of every book of the Bible and numerous other Biblical topics. It is an incredible site that will significantly help you correctly interpret the Bible, discover more about large themes and ideas, and give you a resource to increase your comprehensive Bible knowledge. It's amazing.

With all that said, let me encourage you to regularly open up God's Word with the correct perspective. The most incredibly wise, loving God, creator of the universe, is communicating to you through the Bible. May you always open the Word remembering that God wants to use it to draw you to Him. May you allow Him to transform you to live more like Christ, fulfilling the calling He has placed on you to be a light to the darkness.

Now that you have some tools to navigate your way through the Bible, I want to give you a few more simple instruments to make your reading more productive.

Questions For Reflection:

- How does reading the Bible for the author's intended meaning help you avoid misinterpretation?

- How might discovering the A.I.M. enhance your understanding and application of a passage?

- What did you think about the section on individualism? What issues do you have with a corporate interaction and responsibility to God? Spend time talking to God about that.

- Use your own words to explain the difference between prescriptive and descriptive passages.

- Have you ever used a commentary? Why or why not?

- Look up Tom Constable's Commentary and read his information on Matthew 10:34-36. How did the commentary help clarify these potentially confusing verses?

Chapter 6

S.O.A.P.ing

Have you ever been around someone who talks about the Bible with great enthusiasm, sharing what God has revealed to them through their reading? If you haven't, you should find someone who loves God's Word because it is truly inspiring. The danger, though, is that it can also be discouraging. For many people, the Bible is often a frustrating struggle to get through. The excitement they hear about the "living Word" doesn't reflect their experience of boring words that seem nothing more than decent advice written to an ancient culture. Perhaps that is you, and even though you've been equipped with some things that can enrich your time, you're worried the amount of work it takes to go through everything we've talked about is way too daunting. I want to encourage you not to be discouraged—your Biblical investment will be worth it. I also want to give you a tool which will immediately enhance your time in God's Word. Pray, then S.O.A.P.

I'll discuss what S.O.A.P. stands for in a second, but to help you remember S.O.A.P., think about God's Word in tandem with the benefits of actual soap. Soap cleanses you, makes you smell good, is used every day, and is something you actually have to use to receive its benefits. Without soap, you start to stink, people may avoid you, and if you go long enough, you even begin to be repulsed by yourself. Do you see the correlation? S.O.A.P.ing is a great acronym to remember, not just because it's memorable, but because it reminds you of the benefits of reading—S.O.A.P.ing, in God's Word.

Before you begin to S.O.A.P. in God's Word, prepare your heart and mind by praying for your time to be rich and transformational. If you've got problems focusing, remembering, or staying awake, ask God for strength to get through those struggles. Pray for God to reveal things in your life and about Him that make you want to learn more. Too often, people begin the discipline of study, hoping their willpower will be enough to overcome distractions, only to abandon their commitment a few days, weeks, or months later. God is stronger than your willpower, so ask for God's strength. Ask for a heart that longs for God's Word. Ask for a heart that knows how important study is, even if you don't see results. Ask God to speak to your heart, to help you understand the difficult things. Ask Him to help you practice what you are learning. Praying before you read prepares you to hear what God wants to say. Don't just jump right into a reading, trying to hurry through it. Praying keeps you from this by slowing you down, helping you remember God is communicating with you, and preparing you to be transformed through His Word.

Now that you've prepared your heart in prayer, it's time to begin S.O.A.P.ing. S.O.A.P. is an acronym to remind you how to process your time in God's Word:

- Scripture

- Observation

- Application

- Prayer

The goal of S.O.A.P.ing is to move from merely reading scripture to interacting with it. S.O.A.P.ing will help you correctly interpret, better understand, and transformatively reflect on God's communication with you.

> *God is stronger than your willpower, so ask for God's strength.*

Scripture

Start by reading and writing about the scripture you read. I know this seems a bit redundant to say "read scripture," in a chapter all about studying God's Word, but two important things are being asked of you here.

1. *Start by reading scripture:* Don't start by reading what someone else thinks of scripture or by someone else's reflection on his time in God's Word. If you start with someone else's perspective, you may miss what God is trying to say to you, and you may be skewed to see the scripture in a way it was never intended. Remember, the Bible is God's living Word, and He wants to communicate with you. You may need more information to understand a passage, but start by reading the verses for yourself, not by reading an explanation from someone else. If the Bible is God's main form of communication to you, then seek what He is saying in His Word first, not in a book written *about* His Word. There are many great books, blogs, devotionals, and videos about "The Word," but they shouldn't replace reading the Bible for yourself.

2. *Write down the scripture:* The process of writing it out will slow your mind, allowing you to focus on what is being said, and will enhance your comprehension and memorization. Writing out a whole chapter or chapters can be

daunting, so at least take time to write down a verse that stood out to you or the basic ideas presented in your reading. However you do it, start by reading scripture and practice writing down what you read as a regular part of your time in God's Word.

Observation

Don't rush through it. Often, we quickly forget, or have a hard time comprehending what we've read because we don't take time to really look at the text. When I was in school, I had to write book reports answering questions about the main character, plot, climax, and resolution. I wasn't a big fan of book reports because I always thought, "the teacher knows all this stuff, why does she need to waste her time reading what she already knows?" (I was very concerned for my teacher—okay, my motivation was a bit more self-serving.) Of course, the point of the book report wasn't to benefit the teacher. The reason for the book report was to help me understand what was going on in the story. When I didn't have to write a book report, I'd read the book with a lot less interest, flying through it to gain the big ideas but missing so much of the writing. The sad thing is many of us approach the Bible the same way, satisfied to get the basic idea, but missing so much depth and beauty.

Observation slows you down to notice what can easily be overlooked and dismissed. If writing a book report at the end of each of your readings is helpful, go ahead and do that. The point is not that you have to write a thesis paper on everything you read, but that your reading and comprehension will be significantly enriched by taking the time to observe the following things:

> *Observation slows us down to notice what can easily be overlooked and dismissed.*

- What is the main idea of this text?

- What exactly is happening?

- What problem is being addressed?

- What is the surrounding context?

- What jumps out to you in the passage?

- Who is the author? Who is it written to?

- What's one thing you didn't notice before?

- What seems interesting or unusual?

- What comes before and after the text?

- Is there repetition, comparison, or contrast?

- How does this text fit into the Bible as a whole?

Observation needs to be done carefully because it's easy to misinterpret the answers to these overarching questions based on our own presuppositions. One tool that we've talked about that is very helpful in your observation is having a good commentary. During your observation, be sure to ask God to help you stay true to the A.I.M. (author's intended meaning). Here are some of the more significant questions you can ask and observe.

- Why would God want this included in His Word?

- Why might the author have included this?

- Why are the characters acting this way?

- What encouragement, information, or challenge would the original hearers receive from this?

- What does this say about God?

- What does this say about humans?

Before we go on to the last two steps, I know that observation may seem like way too big a task. It can be frustrating because it's so time-consuming. If you begin to feel this way, let me encourage you that the hard work of asking these questions, and digging deeper, will pay off. You don't need to sit down with a sheet of paper and have all these questions answered before moving on, but these questions should always be on your mind. If writing down the answers helps you, great, but merely having those questions on your mind will force you to read with greater awareness and foster a more in-depth understanding. Lastly, as you observe the scripture, be aware of things that stand out to you because your highlighted observations are a crucial part of moving to the next step.

Application

After you have prayed, read, and observed scripture, you can move to application. Application asks and then responds to this question:

What does this mean for my life, and what action do I need to take?

Like observation, you must be sure that you are responsible to the text in how you apply it to your life. Three of the biggest mistakes I see when seeking the application are:

1. The assumption that descriptive passages are prescriptive. (Like the parable of the rich man we explored earlier)

2. The assumption that prescriptive passages are only descriptive. (i.e., "Flee from all sexual immorality" was for that culture, because of what they were dealing with, not for what I watch on Netflix or HBO." Or "If you're my disciple, you'll do what I command" is dismissed with "disciples are the 12, not me, so I don't have to do all Christ asks.")

3. The assumption of: "I've got my stuff together, and don't really need to deal with this in my life." It's one thing to read God's Word; it's a whole other thing to allow God's Word into the deepest areas of your life to root out all sin. Transformation usually isn't comfortable, so it's easy to excuse attitudes and actions to avoid the change God wants to produce in you.

Now, there may be some of your reading which you can't apply to your life, so don't force an "I have to do this" reaction to those verses. Instead, the application at those times may lead you to a greater understanding of who God is and His incredibly loving plan. Sometimes, because of your own blinders, or lack of understanding, the application can be difficult. That is why having accountability and someone to talk to about your reading is so valuable.

Here are some questions to ask for application:

- What action or attitude might God be trying to mold more like Him through this reading?

- Is there a sin in my life that this is speaking to that I need to repent of and correct?

- Is there something about God that I need to remind myself of through this reading?

- What is the Holy Spirit bringing to my mind that requires some action in my life?

- Is there anyone in my life that God is calling me to share this with?

- How does this change or enhance my understanding and interaction with God? With others?

Prayer

Take what you've processed back to God, praise Him for who He is, talk to Him about the implications of what you just read. Ask Him for the strength to remember what you learned and the power to carry out the application. If you S.O.A.P. in the morning, pray God will use what you learned to guide your interactions throughout the day. Take time to reflect on your dependence on God from the day before. If you read at the end of the day, spend time thinking through your day, praying God will show you how he moved in your life and how your actions reflected Jesus. If you read in the middle of the day, do a little bit of both of these. Ask God to use His Word to transform you to be more like Christ, to understand the hope that He provides, and to be bold in loving others and sharing the Gospel. If there are any personal requests, bring those to Him too.*

*For more, see "Prayer" in the Disciplines section.

While everything we've talked about so far is super helpful, I admit it can still sound a bit like drudgery. I can guarantee that Bible reading won't always be fun, but this next tool changed my entire perspective on Bible reading, helping me be more consistent with my time in God's Word...and it's anything by drudgery.

> *Ask God to use His Word to transform you to be more Christ-like, to understand the hope that He provides, and to be bold in loving others and sharing the Gospel.*

<u>Questions For Reflection:</u>

- Take time to practice S.O.A.P.ing.

- What was the easiest part?

- What was the most challenging part?

- How did this help you focus and gain better retention?

Chapter 7

Keeping Up The Habit

Several years ago, I struggled to make a daily practice of spending time in the Word. I had taught the importance of regularly reading the Bible, and I believed in its significance, but my life didn't reflect that value. Then I led a mission trip to Africa. During the trip, I felt a desperation for God along with a desire to set an example for my team with daily morning devotional time. I decided I'd wake up before breakfast each morning and spend time in the Word and prayer. The first morning was tough. Suffering from jet lag and a late-night, but pushed through, got up, grabbed a big cup of coffee, and went outside to do what I'd committed to. I walked outside with my hot coffee, and the breeze of Africa gently swirled around me. It was cool and crisp enough to wake me up and make me appreciate the warmth the coffee brought. Yet it wasn't so cold that the rising sun couldn't do its work. The temperature was perfect and the sounds of Africa waking up fluttered in and out of my awareness.

I read God's Word in an environment full of green and brown grass, thatched huts, animals scurrying in the far field, and the golden warmth of the sun slowly removing the morning chill. As I finished spending time in God's Word, I remember thinking, "Wow, this was awesome." It was glorious, and from that first morning on, I was excited about waking up early to spend time in God's Word. It was there, in Africa, that I realized time in God's Word can be an excitedly anticipated ritual.

Sadly, many see Bible reading as an unenjoyable task that Christians should do. Maybe the super-spiritual people enjoy it, but most people read unenthused. My time in Africa was an invitation from God to see how enjoyable it could be. So, what's the tool for your Bible study? What should you do? Well, go to Africa, of course...Just kidding (but if you can, I highly recommend it).

Enjoy It

Seriously though, here is my recommendation. Set up your time with God in an environment you really enjoy. Think about your space with God like you would with a good friend. You probably wouldn't like your time with your friends if all you ever did was meet in a cold basement, half asleep, hungry, and needing to get to work. Ideally, you'd want to hang out with your friends while eating, grabbing a drink, or doing something enjoyable. So...do that. If you're a morning person who likes coffee, order your favorite latte, and enjoy it with God. If you like being outside, schedule a regular hike you'll look forward to and go on a walk with God. If you're an evening person who loves dessert, bake brownies at the beginning of the week, and set one (or five) aside for each night, anticipating the delicious brownie you get to eat with

> *Set up your time with God in an environment you really enjoy.*

God. You can do a million things to help make your time with God something you eagerly look forward to.

Will there be times when you just have to be disciplined? Yes, but you have an opportunity to tie your time with God to an element which can elevate expectations, and help you interact with God more richly. I don't get to wake up in Africa every morning, but my time there helped me establish a pattern of regular mornings with God. While I couldn't bring Africa home, I could bring home the experience of waking up to coffee, so I purchased a coffee maker with an automatic brewing timer. This allows me to look forward to waking up to warm, freshly brewed coffee and my time with God.

I've had numerous conversations with people who are struggling to spend time in God's Word. When I ask them about the environment in which they engage God, I'm seldom shocked they are having such a difficult time. Like me, before Africa, time in God's Word is often forced into an environment that is dull, distracting, and difficult. No wonder it's so hard to practice this discipline. A terrible environment can kill interaction and enjoyment, so set up a place where you anticipate meeting with God.

Schedule It

A mentor of mine once told me, "If I want to know what is important in your life, there are two places I'll look—your checkbook and your calendar." This speaks to the difference between a stated value and an actual value. If my

> *"If I want to know what is important in your life, there are two places I'll look—your checkbook and your calendar."*

mentor asked, "What's important to you, Drew?" I could give plenty of answers that I think are important, but how I live my life and spend my money is the revelation of my actual values. In the case of Bible reading, if someone were to take a look at your calendar, how important would they say "spending time with God" is to you?

If reading the Bible is vital, I want to challenge you to schedule your time with God. Put it on your calendar and keep that time sacred. If you're having a hard time regularly being in the Word, don't assume it will naturally happen or that you'll "just make time for it." That may be the very reason you're having a hard time making it an actual value. Other events or a desire to "veg out" often crowd out our time with God if it isn't scheduled. If you look at your schedule and there is no time set aside for God, most likely other things will take up your time.

An excellent time for some people to schedule Bible reading is in the morning before the chaos of the day. Some find their lunch break is when they are most awake, and some prefer evenings, to reflect on their day. There isn't a right time, but there is a wrong time—when it's no time at all. If your boss asked to meet with you, I'm sure you would put it on the calendar, and you wouldn't miss it for 30 more minutes of SportsCenter. God is so much more important than your boss, so you should treat your time with Him with the sacred respect He deserves and not assume you'll find time for Him somewhere in your day. I have found that once I mark the date and times on my calendar and other opportunities come up, my calendar tells me, "no, you can't put anything here; you're busy." Without it, I can almost guarantee my time with God would be crowded out with other, less important things. This leads to my next tool for you.

Consistency

I have never met a mature Christian who doesn't spend regular time studying God's Word. Many people wish they had a deeper, more personal relationship with God, yet don't do the very thing that would help enhance their relationship—spend regular time in God's

Word. Instead, most Christians rely on a once-a-week sermon for their interaction with God's Word. There might be some things you pick up from a sermon-a-week but expecting your relationship with God to grow through a one-hour service on Sunday is like believing a marriage will thrive with spouses who only see each other once a week for a quick coffee break.

Sure, some things can help the relationship in that short time, but one hour a week is hardly a way to significantly grow the relationship. Consistent, committed time in the Word is crucial, no matter what comes up. Committed consistency doesn't mean that if there is an emergency, you tell your kids they need to drive themselves to the E.R. because you're "spending time with God." It does mean you may have to get creative when it seems like all the world's distractions are thrown at you.

This could look like delaying your time, because of the emergency, to later that day. It may mean that you spend five minutes reading and praying instead of 30 minutes. It may mean you listen to the Bible on your phone as you drive your kid to the E.R. Do your best to keep your time consistently sacred, and when life throws you a curveball, try to find a way to still give space to engaging deeper with God.

One of the easiest ways to get off track from regular time with God is by inconsistency with Him. If you only read the Bible once a week, something will come up. A missed day is now a missed two weeks, and if it's been two weeks, why not three, four, fifty-two… Not only that, consistently inputting God's Word protects you from the lies of the world, which are eager to tear you away from the truth.

If you are just starting your discipline of Bible reading, choose a time of day when you are most focused and free from distractions, and set aside 15 minutes to read and reflect. A great way to work consistent Bible reading into your schedule is to look at the days of your week which already have consistency built into them. For instance, if you work Monday through Friday from 8 a.m. until 4 p.m. and have a lunch break at 12, you can schedule your Bible reading Mon-Fri at 6:00 a.m. before you get ready. You could schedule your reading at 12:05 when you've found a place to eat your lunch, or you can choose 4:10 p.m., right after you get off work. I've found that my work schedule's consistency has given me the structure to be more regular in my reading schedule.

Weekends are less structured, so I'm less consistent, but during the workweek, I start the day with my Bible, journal...and coffee. I'll give you more tools for enhancing your reading and reflection in the next section, but those tools won't matter if you aren't engaging in consistently reading God's Word.

Accountability

Have you ever made a commitment to make a life improvement, convinced that you would discipline yourself to accomplish your goal? Many of us do this kind of thinking at the New Year.

'This year, I'm going to save 30% of my paycheck to buy a house in 3 years."

"This year, I'm going to wake up early to kick the habit of sleeping in till 10 a.m."

"This year, I'm going to exercise every day."

"This year, I'm going to stop smoking."

"This year _____ ."

These are all very good things, with great intentions that will benefit your life. Yet, if you're like many people, a few hours, days, or weeks into the year, you've forgotten the passion for your commitment. You've convinced yourself that it's not as important as you thought. Bible reading tends to be another one of these best-intentioned goals which don't make it past a few days or a few weeks. Maybe you go to church or a conference where you are inspired to regularly read God's Word. Maybe you buy a new Bible as an investment to your new commitment, but a month later, it's become the same type of dust collector as your last one.

Scheduling and consistency are great steps to keeping this from happening. However, they both have one inherent problem. They are both dependent on you.

This is why accountability is so crucial. Accountability gives someone else permission to make sure you are as scheduled and consistent as you say you want to be. Accountability is a great thing to help keep you on track and help keep you from 'another great intention, unfulfilled.' An accountability partner can challenge you to live the values you claim, clarify things you don't understand, and help you see what God is doing in and through you.

Schedule and consistency are also keys to accountability. It's a good idea to have an accountability partner who you see regularly and who follows up consistently. Set up a weekly time to check in. Find someone you can trust, someone who won't be afraid to call you on your excuses when you say, "I just didn't have time this week."

> *An accountability partner can challenge you to live the values you claim, clarify things you don't understand, and help you see what God is doing in and through you.*

Baloney! Remember, you're not hiring a drill sergeant, to keep you in line (although they may have to). An accountability partner is someone who can be tough when needed, gentle when needed, and who has a desire to see you grow in your relationship with God.

Community Reading

Discussing your reading in a community can motivate you to stay consistent, deepen your understanding, and encourage transformation. Reading and dialoguing in community provides the benefit of hearing perspectives from others that can enhance your reading.

One of the reasons God has called His people to be the church is because there is a dynamic interplay of understanding and growth which can only happen in community. In First Corinthians 12, Paul speaks about the church like a body—we are incredibly dependent on one another because we each have different gifts to be used to glorify God. This applies to Bible reading too. There are life stories, perspectives, talents, and personalities that God gives each person to use for one another.

As others share how the reading affected them, you will see things you've never seen before and see how personal God is in His communication. I'm always astounded when I discuss the Bible with other believers because what others see in the passages and where God is challenging them adds to my understanding of God. Our conversations expose how living, dynamic, and amazing His Word is. In the same way, what you share can encourage and inspire others.

There is also great value in asking your questions in community. The Bible can be confusing and the ability to discuss your questions is pivotal to learning. If you never dialogue about your reading with anyone, you'll probably remain confused, and you'll definitely miss an opportunity to grow.

When I was studying to be a teacher, there was a common saying; "You don't know it until you teach it." Every time you talk about what you read you are, in a way, teaching it, and with that, you are gaining more knowledge. I'm not saying you have to teach a class on everything you read, but when you ask questions and talk about what you read, not only will you have your questions answered, but your understanding will expand too. How cool is that! So, don't read the Bible (just) on your own. Find a Jesus-loving, others-serving, Bible-teaching church to invest in. A good church community will increase your Biblical understanding and allow you to learn in community to live out your faith.

> *"You don't know it until you teach it."*

Your time in the Word can be exciting, enriching, and transformative. In those times, praise God for a heart that eagerly S.O.A.P.s and an interaction that fills you up. Bible reading can also be difficult and dull. In those times, pray that God will help you continue the discipline of S.O.A.P.ing. No matter how you're feeling, thank him for the times where S.O.A.P.ing has been enriching and ask him to increase the sweetness of your time. By S.O.A.P.ing, along with accountability, scheduled consistency, community, and enjoyment, the opportunity to grow to be more like Christ will expand, and your relationship with God will be developed in substantial ways. What could be better than that?

A Key Reminder

I want to end this section by reminding you of how we began our discussion on Bible reading. Don't read the Bible just so you can be a more educated, smarter Christian. If you read the Bible like a textbook, filling your head with knowledge about God without it moving you to more deeply knowing God, you're missing the point. Transformation, not merely head knowledge, is God's desire for you as you consume His Word, but here's the kicker—the Bible doesn't cause transformation.... WHAT?? I thought the intent of God's Word is transformation? It is, but not the way that is often thought. God's Word's primary goal is to introduce you to and help develop your relationship with God. It is not God's Word that transforms us. It is God Himself. God is living and relational, loves you, and wants

to be the center of your life. For you to look more like Him in love, joy, peace, patience, kindness, self-control, goodness, and gentleness, you must allow Him to shape and direct your life as you read His Word.

> *It is not God's Word that transforms us. It is God Himself.*

Imagine for a second that you are in a long-distance friendship with the most incredible, wisest friend in the world. You regularly receive lengthy text messages of encouragement and wisdom. This friend tells you about her day, her hopes for the future, and also is caringly honest with you when you've screwed up and need correcting. Because of her love and friendship, you read her text messages with interest and allow her critique to change the way you act. The reason that you continue to communicate with her, even when it's difficult, is that the person on the other side of the texts is someone you trust, know, and love.

Now imagine all those texts having come from unknown numbers, from random strangers. The words may be exactly the same, but the meaning of each text is pointedly different. While there may be some helpful and encouraging truths, your interaction with the text messages would suffer. First, you would be skeptical of whatever was written, and second, the advice and correction would probably become very frustrating. This is how some people approach the Bible: focusing on the words written and not knowing the God behind them. Like your text messages, there are things that you can learn from your reading that will change your life, but real transformation comes from the loving relationship you have with the person on the other side.

When we approach the text (The Bible) as advice to apply to transform our lives, we miss the point of the Bible—God's Word, inviting us into a deeper relationship with Him...the one who transforms our lives.

Questions For Reflection:

- What is the most challenging part of spending regular time in God's Word?

- What can you do to enhance your enjoyment of reading the Bible?

- Who in your life has been an example of consistently inputting God's Word into their life?

- Do you have someone in your life who you can regularly talk to about your reading and what God is doing in you? If so, what value have you found in being able to have those discussions? If no, how will you seek out this opportunity?

> *When we approach the text (The Bible) as advice to apply to transform our lives, we miss the point of the Bible—God's Word, inviting us into a deeper relationship with Him...the one who transforms our lives.*

- How can you keep a perspective of approaching God's Word to know Him, and not just to "read the Bible" or "know the Bible"?

PART TWO

Engaging With God In Other Ways (Spiritual Disciplines)

By far, my favorite classes in school were the ones where learning was interactive and engaged more than just my mind. I clearly remember 4th-grade social studies on the California gold rush. During the weeks we spent on this topic, we studied the pioneers' excitement and hardships. We were placed in groups of four and had to complete tasks to earn "gold." One of the projects was to create a diorama of a pioneer home and setting. After we were given the assignment, I walked home with a lofty goal and talked to my Dad about building something beyond my teacher's expectations.

It wasn't long after that we went to the craft store, purchasing a handful of wooden dowels and other equipment. In the garage, my dad and I worked on completing the plans to create an amazing log cabin. We cut and notched each dowel to sit precisely on top of one another. We found rocks in our yard, and hot glued them on a cardboard frame to emulate a fireplace and chimney. We used small strips of leather for the door hinges and layered thinly cut balsa wood to make a perfect roof. We completed the cabin by adding a stain to make it look authentic. The whole process enveloped me and drew me into the learning experience.

While my teacher would have been able to get through the curriculum more quickly if we only read the textbook, the experiences built around our learning made it so much more personal, fun, engaging, and meaningful. The next things we'll talk about are activities that can help you interact with God in the same way.

Discipline (Again)

Everything we will talk about in this section can make your interaction with God more profound. But keep in mind the following practices are called "Spiritual Disciplines" for a reason. They are activities you should engage in regularly, even when your excitement and desires wanes. As Paul says in First Corinthians 9, "All athletes are disciplined in their training. They do it to win a prize that will fade away, but we do it for an eternal prize. So, I run with purpose in every step. I am not just shadowboxing. I discipline my body like an athlete, training it to do what it should. Otherwise, I fear that after preaching to others I myself might be disqualified" (vv. 25-27) The Christian walk is one in which fierce discipline benefits you. It prepares you for the work God has called you to. It builds character. It allows your witness to others to be more robust. It should not be something we do only "when I feel like it." It should be a regular engagement to ensure that, when testing, hardships, questions, and judgment comes, your foundation is strong enough to carry you through.

You may be in a season where the closeness of God is so tangible that you eagerly engage in these disciplines—they seem less like disciplines and more like joyful opportunities. If that is you, great! Make sure you thank God for the ability to practice these disciplines with joy and make sure you share that joy with others.

On the other hand, you may be in a season where discipline is precisely the right word. You don't want to do any of these, and every time you try, it's just more frustrating. If that is you, I just want to cheer you on, "Keep going, you got this!!" Ask God to give you the strength to keep practicing these disciplines, and don't lose focus on the fact that there will be a payoff if you keep at them. It may not be for a while, but there will be a time when you look back and realize just how formative your commitment to these disciplines have been.

Chapter 8

Church

Before I even entered the building, I was warmly greeted with a loving enthusiasm, which made me know the excitement I felt was real. Approaching the entrance, a handful more people offered their "welcomes," and a few introduced themselves to me and asked if they could help me find my way. Once inside the lobby, I witnessed groups gathered in small communities, some laughing, some talking about the latest football game, some more serious, some crying and praying together. In each group, there was a palpable love. Someone called me over, eager to know me and help me feel connected.

When the service started, the sound of voices unashamedly giving praise to God filled the space. When the announcements came, I was shocked to hear an affirmation because "All serving opportunities were overflowing with volunteers, and there was a greater desire to serve than opportunities to do so." When the service ended, ten different people came up to me and invited me to lunch. I had to decline each one, but as I made my way to the exit, I noticed most of the congregation remained, either conversing or huddled in small groups praying together. I asked someone close to me if the groups were something you signed up to be part of and was told, "No, those groups just spring up organically, in an awareness of the needs of those around them and a desire for God's Work to be done in this church."

I had never witnessed a church that was so full of love, aware of others, participating in what God was doing, in tune with the Spirit's moving, so full of servants... And then I woke up. Oh, how I wish my dream would come true. Don't you?

To be this type of church, let me remind you "The Church" is not a building. The church is a gathering of people focused on God and doing God's work. There are two main ways the New Testament authors refer to the church: "Christ's Bride" and "The Body of Christ." By those two descriptions, three things should be clear.

1. Jesus loves the church.

2. The church is extremely important to God.

3. As a follower of Christ, it is crucial to participate in the church to express the fullness of Christ's love to others.

Despite these pretty obvious conclusions, many people believe participation in the church is only minimally important. Even though this is common thinking today, throughout history, dismissing yourself from participating in the church body has been seen as entirely contradictory to following Christ.

As I talk about 'the discipline of 'church," you need to understand this is about more than just regularly attending Sunday services. The 'discipline of church' is primarily a participatory discipline, not an observing discipline.

Regularly attending church may deepen your relationship with God and should provide opportunities to connect with other Christians, but if your participation in the church ends when the service ends, then you're missing out on a HUGE part of what the church is supposed to be. The 'Church' is God's people doing God's work. Here is what participating in the "discipline of church" looks like.

Supernatural Love Of Each Other

Hours before His crucifixion, Jesus washed His disciples' feet, a disgusting task, reserved for servants. And yet, the God of the universe washed the feet of men who will aban-

> *The 'Church' is God's people doing God's work.*

don Him, deny Him, and betray Him. He lowered Himself to the place of a servant, expressing supernatural, sacrificial love. After Jesus washed their feet, Judas left the room, and Jesus told the remaining disciples, "So now I am giving you a new commandment: Love each other. Just as I have loved you, you should love each other. Your love for one another will prove to the world that you are my disciples." (Jn. 13: 34-35).

The command Jesus gives here is supernatural love—love that goes beyond human reason. In this case, the object of that love is "one another." In other words, there is a way Christians should love each other which sets them apart in an audaciously humble way. The way God has chosen to most clearly express His love through you, is in and through His Church. While there is an individual calling on each person's life, the individual calling is to participate in extreme love in Christ's corporate movement.

As a follower of Christ, you have a responsibility to other believers. If you believe Jesus rose from the dead and you've decided to follow Him, the calling is the same for you. Love one another in such a way that others will know you follow Christ. Saying you're a Christ-follower and not being part of a church is like saying you're on a hockey team and never interacting with your teammates. Two of the most obvious ways to tell if someone is actually on a team are their participation with the team and their play in the game. Maybe you've convinced yourself you're on the team but wearing a jersey and actually being on the team are very different.

> *There is a way Christians should love each other which sets them apart in an audaciously humble way.*

The church should be a community that rallies around you when things get tough, prays for you, helps you see the daily grace of God, surrounds you with people who continually remind you of the Gospel, and challenges you to live for Jesus. But the church is not just "for you," it calls something "from you." The church should be a place where you rally around others when things get tough, pray for others, help others see the daily grace of God, and continually remind others of the Gospel. It's a place where YOU help people to live for Jesus. The church doesn't need you so their membership can be higher or so you can be a "good Christian." You need to be in the church because a relationship with God can't be disconnected from a relationship with God's people. "God's people, doing God's work" means we are unified by the God who came down to express the most incredible love ever, a love we're to show to one another.

> *The church is not just "for you," it calls something "from you."*

Do you participate in the life of the church in a way that others know you love Jesus?

Using Your Gifts

We'll look into the gifts God has given you to participate in His Church in the chapter about spiritual gifts, but in this section, you need to know that using your gifts is indispensable to fully expressing the character of Christ to the world. In First Corinthians 12 Paul, reminds and admonishes Christians about their participation in the church. He uses an analogy of the church being "the body of Christ." Amid Paul's explanation about each person having unique gifts, he makes this strong statement; "The eye can never say to the hand, 'I don't need you.' The head can't say to the feet, 'I don't need you.'" How did you read that verse right now? My guess is how I've read it for many years—Paul is gently explaining that one part of the body can't say to another, "I don't need you." While that is partly true, I think there is also a firmer tone that can be read from this statement.

Re-read it, but this time as a rebuke toward the elements that are saying, "I don't need you." When read in this new way, Paul's passionate disagreement with those who

> *YOU CANNOT SAY,*
> *"Church, I don't need you,"*
> *or "Church, you don't*
> *need me."*

say, "I don't need the church," is: "NO! YOU CAN'T SAY THAT! SAYING, 'I DON'T NEED YOU,' MAKES NO SENSE." The church is the bride of Christ, the physical expression of Christ to the world. This is of utmost importance, and as a Christ-follower, YOU CANNOT SAY, "Church, I don't need you," or "Church, you don't need me." By serving in and participating as 'The Church,' you fulfill part of your God-given role and help expand His Kingdom. You reveal to the world to the beautiful, redeeming, life-changing hope of Christ. Yes, the church has messed up too often, but that doesn't mean our collective responsibility to one another, or the world, is removed. You cannot say to the body of Christ, "I do not need you."

Practicing The Discipline: Find a church, get connected, and start serving.

Find A Church

If you aren't part of a church, find a Bible-teaching, Jesus-loving, difference-making church, and get involved. Ask trusted Christians for church recommendations and ask them to pray with you as you seek out a new church community. When finding a church, look at core beliefs and don't be afraid to ask a staff member or someone in leadership to help you understand the church's vision and values. Ask a lot of questions. Don't be afraid to try a few different churches until you find a place where you can grow, serve, and participate in expanding God's Kingdom.

When Tension Rise...And They Will

Whether you already have a church or are looking for one, there will be a time when you become frustrated with the church (it could take months or decades, but something will cause frustration). This section may feel like a tangent from the spiritual discipline of going to church, but the ability to faithfully walk through tensions with your church could be one of the biggest exercises of this discipline. If you are part of a church that strives to love God, follow Jesus, and lovingly builds God's Kingdom, praise God and participate in what God is doing there. If, on the other hand, you find yourself at a church that doesn't seem to desire to be the full expression of God's love, or whose method of accomplishing God's calling is something with which you disagree, there are ways to remain faithful to the discipline of 'church' while being responsible to how God might be challenging you.

1. Be The Catalyst For Change

Too many people love to talk about what is wrong with their church without doing anything about it. If you see a place where your church is lacking, instead of going to the pastor and saying, "You need to do this," how about saying, "I need to do this." Remember, there are many parts of the body, and each has its function. Maybe improvements you see are obvious to you because you are the part of the body God is calling to invest in that area of the church. Don't complain about what needs to change; be the answer to the change you want to see. A couple of words of caution:

a. If this is an idea or an improvement you want to introduce to your pastor, be loving and gentle in how you approach him. I'm assuming he has a lot on his plate and his heart. Don't go in with guns blazing about what is wrong with the church and how you will fix it; that could end up doing more harm than the good you intend.

b. Your willingness to help the church look more like Christ is a good and noble desire, but not every idea you have can be something the "church does." Don't take offense at that. For example: Let's say you want to start a prayer night. This is an excellent thing, and what could be better than fostering a heart of prayer? But if you're told, "We can't host your event at the church, and won't be able to announce it," it's easy to hear the lie: "The church just doesn't care about prayer."

If the church is "God's people, doing God's work," why do you have to wait for a church announcement and space to accomplish what God has placed on your heart? Perhaps there are other restrictions you don't know about (limitation of announcements, space was already promised to someone else, etc.). A "no" doesn't necessarily mean that the church doesn't support it or that you can't do it. It may just mean you'll need to find a more organic way to organize people around this idea. If you get a "no," my suggestion would be to lovingly ask, "why?" If the reason is reasonable, then a great next question is, "how might I be able to make this work?"

> *If the church is "God's people, doing God's work," why do you have to wait for a "church announcement and space" to accomplish what God has placed on your heart?*

The solution may look very different from what you had pictured, but if it's as important as you've said, then that shouldn't stop you. You might need to adjust your plans and start the prayer night in your living room with a group of your friends, inviting others to participate by word of mouth.

As you involve yourself in a church community, I can guarantee a time will come when there will be frustration, things you would do differently, or personalities you just don't like. None of these are necessarily reasons to leave. They may be the very things God is using to grow and stretch you. If you try to be a catalyst for positive, God-glorifying, impacting change, and the church asks you not to engage in any of the improvements you want to help make, it may be time to move on to the next step.

2. Find A New Church

Committed, desperate prayer and counsel should occur before taking this next step. If you've done those things and God has released you to explore a new community, then do so with continued prayer. I can't stress this enough—leaving comes after you have attempted to improve your community and after significant prayer. Both these actions should be done with great humility and love.

Finding a different church, in this case, is not a bad thing. Serving in a new church community where you can use your gifts and connect more deeply can be a great opportunity to ignite your faith in a new way.

Wherever you find yourself, you need to engage in the discipline of being part of a church—not just attending— but serving and getting connected. I've been a part of a church since I was born, and I've seen people go through the highest highs and lowest lows. The people who put in the hard work of getting

> *Wherever you find yourself, you need to engage in the discipline of being part of a church—not just attending but serving and getting connected.*

connected benefit from a support system through all of life's circumstances. Their investment creates a connection of people who know them well enough to rally around them and celebrate in the good times, cry in the tough times, and pray for them all the time. Sadly, too many people don't invest, don't form community, and eventually become angry with a church that "lacks support." Often, those who are frustrated, jealously witness the support others receive, not realizing the significant time and effort it took to make the loving, supportive connections. Community and connection are hard work and take a lot of effort.

The discipline of 'church' goes far beyond an hour and a half on Sunday. Involve yourself in serving somewhere, make an intentional effort to build relationships and invest in others. Even when you don't feel like it, make church a regular part of your life. When you do, you may just find you are more connected than ever before, and your relationship with God is growing deeper. As a Christ-follower, you can't say, "I don't want to be a part of God's people... His Church." Instead, you are to be part of a community of people who love each other with pursuant, sacrificial, Christ-centered love.

Questions For Reflection:

- What is the most challenging part about getting connected?

- What can you do to discipline yourself to be more known and to know others more?

- What areas of serving can you involve yourself in the church?

- What is keeping you from greater involvement?

- How can you participate in being a supernaturally loving community?

Chapter 9

Worship

"Men are made to worship, to bow down and adore in the presence of the Mystery inexpressible." —AW Tozer[1]

A few years ago, I led a young adult community, and we went on a retreat up to the mountains. One evening was set aside for a worship night. 60 people were crammed into a small room with a guitar, drums, piano, and vocalists. The young adults were eager to express their love for God. The passion, emotion, and unabandoned willingness to sing as loud as their hearts wanted, gave the evening a truly heavenly feeling. That worship night remains the best worship experience I've ever had. I love to sing, and I love to express my worship of God through music.

As I talk about the discipline of worship, you may be like me, or you could find "worship" to be one of Christianity's most awkward practices. Perhaps you dislike singing and any emotive expression. Raised hands, rocking back and forth, kneeling, shouting, or having your eyes closed all make you slightly (or incredibly) uncomfortable.

More Than Music

However you interact with worship, I've got good news; worship is so much more than the music time at church. *Webster's Dictionary* says worship is "to honor with extravagant love and extreme submission."[2] *Christianity Today* expands on the definition. "True worship…is defined by the priority we place on who God is in our lives and where God is on our list of priorities."[3]

In both definitions singing and music aren't even mentioned. That doesn't mean worship can't involve singing, but it does mean worship is a mindset and a decision to give reverence to God. It's placing God in the right perspective and living according to that. This simply means that everything you do can be an act of worship if it's done intentionally to give God glory and honor Him. Making macaroni and cheese? That could just be a menial task to get food in your stomach, OR you could spend that time worshiping God by thanking Him for the deliciousness of fake cheese, the ability to cook over a stove, and celebrating the fact that God could have made food flavorless but decided not to. Ordering a coffee at Starbucks? That could just be a boring part of your morning routine, OR you could worship God by intentionally seeing the barista as one of God's beloved children, asking her how she is doing, attempting to show her genuine care because you want to use your life to reflect God's love. In each of these cases, there is an approach to life that worships God in everything: placing God in His proper authority of your life and promoting, thanking, praising, and being obedient to Him.

Now, you may argue that parts of these interactions seem like service, not worship, and to that, I would say, "You're right." Setting aside time to have a discussion with a co-worker or friend or making a meal for your family are acts of service, but service and worship work in harmony with each other. Billy Graham said it well when he stated, "The highest form of worship is the worship of unselfish Christian service."[4] Service is worship when you do so in a way that brings God glory.

But I have even more good news; singing and service still aren't the only ways to worship. You can also worship God with how you work and play...and this plays out for eternity.

Heaven's Forever Singing

If you grew up in a Christian home, you've probably heard we will worship God forever in heaven. The picture that used to come to my mind when I heard this was a never-ending choir recital. If you're anything like me, that isn't the most thrilling thing. Like I said before, I love to sing, but even my passion couldn't keep me from being a little bummed that I have to sing forever. My idea of eternal worship has changed as I've learned more about God. I do think there will be plenty of singing in heaven, and it will be so beautiful we'll never want it to stop, but "eternally worshiping God" means quite a bit more than singing. I believe the way we engage in everything we do in heaven will be worship (work, building relationships, playing games, creating art, etc.). All our impure motivations and attitudes will be removed. Each one of our actions will be beautified in a full expression of worship.

> *"Eternally worshiping God" means quite a bit more than singing.*

No longer will I just play hockey because it's fun and a great exercise. I will play hockey, fully realizing how amazing it is that God gave me the ability to play. I will worship as I compete in an appreciation of God's creativity and His physical laws which made ice, pucks, sticks, and skates possible. I will play in gratitude for my teammates and the other team in the unique way God has made them, seeing them with the full love of God. I'll worship God as I hit the puck into the back of the net, thanking Him for the thrill of competition. Not just hockey, but everything that I do will be kept clean from selfishness, anger, and pride. Because of that, I'll be able to realize that every moment in heaven is an incredible gift to be used to thank God and show Him how great I think He is. In short: it will all be worship. Unlike my early assumptions of a tedious choir recital, I look forward to worshipping God in all I do, for eternity.

This heavenly perspective isn't something that will arrive when you die. Your eternal worship starts now. You can bring your worship of God into all aspects of your life.

Do you like running? How might you allow running to be a time where you worship God?

Do you have a job? How can you spend your time at work, aware of God's presence, dedicating your work to Him?

How can your time with your family be an intentional reflection of God, bringing Him glory?

How can each area of your life give God honor with extravagant love and extreme submission?

All this is worship.

Evaluating Worship

We live in a culture that has placed feelings and emotions at the center of how we evaluate the world. Feelings are "truth," and if something doesn't produce an emotional connection, then it isn't worth our time. Without going into a social critique of how hazardous it is to base our lives strictly on our emotions, you need to be aware of how this mentality could affect your interaction with the discipline of worship.

Many Christians have fallen into the trap of evaluating the value of a "worship experience" solely on how it makes them feel. By God's grace, there are times where you may experience God in profound, heart-thrilling ways, but if your emotions become the standard expectation, then you are becoming more drawn to a certain feeling than to God Himself—a far cry from what worship is supposed to be. Worship is about showing God extravagant love and submission, not receiving an overwhelming sense of feeling loved by God. Yes, that may happen, but it is dangerous to enter into worship for what you get. When you do that, you unintentionally make yourself the focus of the worship.

> *Many Christians have fallen into the trap of evaluating the value of a "worship experience" solely on how it makes them feel.*

There is another danger to a mindset that expects some emotional response for worship to be valuable. Perhaps you've talked to people who connect with God on an emotional level which has you questioning if something is wrong with you (since you don't 'feel' like that). Let me just caution and encourage you. The caution is this—there may be something wrong that you need to take care of. Take time to evaluate your life and ask if there are any sins you haven't dealt with that may be holding you back from connecting more deeply with God. If you've evaluated yourself, asked close friends to do the same, allowed the Holy Spirit to reveal sin, and are coming up with nothing, then let me encourage you: There is nothing wrong with you.

Many people aren't moved to emotions in worship. Continue to sing, work, play, enjoy life... as worship to God. It's not about feelings; it's about posturing your heart in thankfulness and praise towards God. It is a beautiful experience to worship God and deeply sense His presence, but worship is a commitment to honor, love, and submit, not a commitment to feel, sense, and be thrilled. With a correct understanding of worship, defining "good worship" changes from "How does it emotionally affect me?" to "How I am honoring, loving, and submitting to God?"

> *Worship is a commitment to honor, love, and submit, not a commitment to feel, sense, and be thrilled.*

Lastly, worship is a discipline you have to practice regularly. Worship calls you back to the truth of who God is and your relationship to Him. It reminds you that He deserves more honor, love, and submission than you could ever give Him. It connects you to the truth that you were created to worship Him in everything you do. For Christ-followers, worship is not an option. First Chronicles 16:23-30 is one of many statements calling those who believe in God to give Him the worship He deserves.

"Let the whole earth sing to the Lord! Each day proclaim the good news that he saves. Publish his glorious deeds among the nations. Tell everyone about the amazing things he does. Great is the Lord! He is most worthy of praise! He is to be feared above all gods. The gods of other nations are mere idols, but the Lord made the heavens! Honor and majesty surround him; strength and joy fill his dwelling. O nations of the world, recognize the Lord, recognize that the Lord is glorious and strong. Give to the Lord the glory he deserves! Bring your offering and come into his presence. Worship the Lord in all his holy splendor. Let all the earth tremble before him. The world stands firm and cannot be shaken."

When you sing songs in response to His love, when you work hard for God, when you interact with others acknowledging God's goodness and presence, when you play with thankful joy, you are worshipping God.

Heaven will be a place of eternal worship in everything you do. While on earth, you prepare yourself for eternity by intentionally engaging in worship. Sometimes worship is through music, sometimes through silent reflection, always through the way you interact with the world around you. May you continually look for opportunities to show God extravagant love and submission—to worship Him.

Questions For Reflection:

- What is the best worship experience you've had? Why would you qualify as "the best"?

- Have you had any seasons in your life where you didn't feel like worshipping God? Explain.

- What helped you proceed through that "blockage" to worship?

- What does it look like for you to worship God outside the weekend church gathering? In your work? At home?

- How do you best engage in worship?

- How can you engage in worship with the extreme love and submission God deserves?

Chapter 10

Prayer

There are a few people in my life who love to pray. I'm not just talking about people who always volunteer to pray when asked, but people who eagerly spend time speaking to God through prayer. These "pray-ers" always appear to have an interaction with God that is transformative—where they hear from Him and where they connect with God in such a way that makes me a little jealous. My prayer life often feels like a one-way monologue. The difference between my prayer life and theirs often has me questioning: If God is so eager to communicate with me, why do some people have a vibrant prayer life while mine tends to be dull? I desire to commune with God through prayer. So, what is missing?

Perhaps my frustration rings true with you. If not, praise God for the ability to connect with Him through prayer. Wherever you find yourself, it is undeniable that prayer is a vital part of your relationship with God. In this chapter, we'll look at how your per-spective of prayer may be hindering your interaction with God. Then I'll give you some tools to think through and engage in to help ignite regular, transformational prayer conversations with God.

How Often Should We Pray?

In his letter to the church in Ephesus, Paul says, "Pray in the Spirit at all times and on every occasion. Stay alert and be persistent in your prayers for all believers everywhere" (Eph. 6:18). And in a letter to the church in Thessalonica, He tells the church to "pray without ceasing" (1 Thess. 5:17, ESV). These two statements high-light the extreme importance of prayer. Out of all the disciplines, this is the only one you are called to do "without ceasing." The com-mand is for something vastly more than your dinner prayers. But what does "at all times" and "without ceasing" really mean? If you are to be obedient to God's Word, does that mean that you need to quit your job, fold your hands, and bow your head every waking moment? Does it mean that before you change your tires or watch a movie, you pause for prayer?

In his book *A Testament of Devotion*, Thomas Kelly answers what it looks like to continuously commune with God.

"There is a way of ordering our mental life on more than one level at once. On one level we may be thinking, discussing, seeing, calculating, meeting all the demands of external affairs. But deep within, behind the scenes, at a more profound level, we may also be in prayer and adoration, song and worship, and a gentle receptive-ness to divine breathing."[1]

"A gentle receptiveness to divine breathing." This is why prayer is so important. "Never ceasing prayer" is making your mind available to God to convict, correct, encourage, and guide you at all moments. This perspective of prayer doesn't mean you eliminate your prayer time; those times can be anchors to call your focus back to your praise and dependence on God. It does mean prayer should not just start with "Dear God" and end with "Amen." It should begin with your alarm and end with your snoring.

God With Mine Or Mine With God's?

One of the main frustrations with prayer stems from the incorrect perspective of what prayer is for. Many people see prayer as an attempt to align God's heart with their own. If you were to review your prayers, would most of them be about asking God for things? Money, a new job, health, etc. Maybe a little bit of "thanks," sprinkled in? The truth is a lot prayers revolve around "asking for stuff."

While petitioning God is not a bad thing (see Phil. 4:6), when it becomes the main thing, it can draw you into a false expectation that prayer is about getting God to do what you want. If the focus of your prayers is only telling God what you need and trying to convince Him to do your bidding, then prayer seems like a complete waste of time in light of Matthew 6:8, "Your Father knows what you need before you ask Him" (NIV). Why pray if He already knows? Either prayer is unnecessary, and you should stop, or this understanding of prayer is incorrect.

Prayer's chief focus is not about convincing God to align His heart with ours. It is instead primarily about aligning our hearts with God. This perspective doesn't eliminate the "asks," but it reframes the prayer toward knowing Him more, allowing Him to transform you, and desiring His will to be done. Richard

> *Prayer's chief focus is not about convincing God to align His heart with ours. It is instead primarily about aligning our hearts with God.*

Foster states, "In prayer, real prayer, we begin to think God's thoughts after Him: to desire the things He desires, to love the things He loves. Progressively we are taught to see things from His point of view."[2] This way of thinking about prayer should completely change how prayer is approached. You may present your request to God, but your prayers should revolve around seeking what God wants in everything.

The paramount need in your life is a deeper understanding of God's love and a life which reflects that love. Yes, getting a new job or having the cancer go away would be great, but your prayers for should be soaked in a desire for God to be glorified and for you to be drawn closer to Him.

> *The paramount need in your life is a deeper understanding of God's love and a life which reflects that love.*

What Jesus Taught

Let's look at how Jesus teaches us to pray and then break it down to help engage God in a more intentional, correct perspective and dialogue. Before we do that, I need to point out that the prayer Jesus prays is meant to set a pattern to help us pray, not be a memorized stanza that we quote every day as our only prayer. Jesus says, "Pray like this," not "Pray this exact prayer." There is value in learning this prayer and reciting it, but remember, God wants to interact with you, not just hear you give a memorized monologue.

"Pray like this: Our Father in heaven, may your name be kept holy. May your Kingdom come soon. May your will be done on earth, as it is in heaven. Give us today the food we need, and forgive us our sins, as we have forgiven those who sin against us. And don't let us yield to temptation, but rescue us from the evil one" (Matthew 6:9-13).

A quick read of this passage may seem to reinforce the idea that prayer is a monologue of requests, but as you'll see, there is so much more going on here. This prayer patterns itself towards a deeper conversation with God and an alignment of the pray-er's heart (you) to God's heart.

Talking With God

Jesus starts the prayer with an affirmation of who God is. *"Our Father in heaven, may your name be kept holy."* These words are not rote and ritualistic blabber. They are an intentional starting point for beginning prayer. Acknowledging God's authority and holiness focuses your heart and mind on Him. Prayer should start by recognizing who God is. The all-powerful, all-knowing, all-loving God of creation is listening to you. With this in mind, prayer should be approached with a holy reverence that invites His transformational power to shape your life.

The next part affirms God's plan and elevates His will above everything else. *"May your Kingdom come soon. May your will be done on earth, as it is in heaven."* This second statement speaks of your intention to align your heart with God's, not twisting God's arm to do what you want. "Your Kingdom come, Your will be done" is also a participatory proclamation. Jesus is teaching you to pray in such a way that says, "God, above all my wants and desires, above all the things that I think, I want you to be King of my life. I want to participate in building your Kingdom now." Praying with this intention reminds you to center your life on joining in God's will. As you pray through the affirmation of God's holiness and for His Kingdom to come, you echo the truth of who God is and place yourself under God's authority.

After you have centered your focus on God, you present your requests, ask for forgiveness, and pray for protection. All of these are done in response to who God is with a supreme desire to have God's Kingdom promoted. *"Give us today the food we need, and forgive us our sins, as we have forgiven those who sin against us. And don't let us yield to temptation, but rescue us from the evil one."* Each of these requests has more to do with a dependence on God than God making your dreams come true. The provision for daily bread is both an ask for sustenance and an affirmation that God is your sustainer. The appeal for forgiveness reflects on where you have failed, requests God's gracious forgiveness, and asks for His help in extending forgiveness to others. Asking for "deliverance from temptation" is a plea to God for spiritual protection and strength. It's an admittance that you can't resist temptation in your own power.

For God's Kingdom to be more fully lived out, you need Him as your source of strength. Requests aren't a shopping list of things God can do for you; they should carry with them an admission of a need for Him that draws you back to a grander understanding of His power and His call on your life.

Now that you know a little bit more about how to pattern and think through your prayers, praying should be a lot easier, and your conversations with God will be full of life, right? Unfortunately, the whole "God is not physically in front of you" thing still makes interacting with Him difficult. Don't be discouraged, though; there are tools that you can use to help your prayer time be more fruitful.

Don't Just Talk... Listen

Perhaps you've had this thought: "Whenever I pray, all that happens is I think thoughts or say something out loud, hoping that God hears me, yet I never get a response..." You're not alone in this frustration. True prayer is speaking to and listening to God. The talking part of prayer is easy; the listening is hard. If aligning your heart to God is the primary focus of prayer, listening should be central to your prayer life. The Dutch philosopher and theologian Soren Kierkegaard put it this way. "A man prayed, and at first, he thought that prayer was talking. But he became more and more quiet until in the end he realized that prayer is listening."[3]

Being able to listen in prayer comes from a belief that God's Holy Spirit is living inside you and wants to guide you. God is not a distant being who is busy with more important things. Jesus promises that God's Spirit will live inside you when you accept Him as your Savior. While you

> *Being able to listen in prayer comes from a belief that God's Holy Spirit is living inside you and wants to guide you.*

may not see a physical manifestation of the Spirit when you decide to follow Jesus, the first Christians experienced the impartation of the Holy Spirit in a pretty incredible way.

"On the day of Pentecost, all the believers were meeting together in one place. Suddenly, there was a sound from heaven like the roaring of a mighty windstorm, and it filled the house where they were sitting. Then, what looked like flames or tongues of fire appeared and settled on each of them. And everyone present was filled with the Holy Spirit and began speaking in other languages, as the Holy Spirit gave them this ability" (Acts 2:1-4).

Here, in the book of Acts, Luke describes the moment the Holy Spirit was delivered to followers of Jesus. God's Spirit was manifested by an ability to speak foreign languages so they could exalt and proclaim God's truth. This account shows the ushering in of a brand-new paradigm—God personally interacts with all those who have chosen to follow Him. Although God's presence in your life may not be revealed in speaking different languages, that doesn't mean He is any less involved in communicating with and through you. The implication of this on your prayer life cannot be ignored— God is not a god that "may pay attention to us sometimes." He is a God who knows His people and wants to be actively involved in their lives for His glory. You and I can communicate with God on a moment-by-moment basis, but our interaction with God depends on our willingness to listen to Him.

There are many methods you can use to listen to God as you pray. However, all must have a firm foundation on what we know is God's primary form of communication with us—His Word, the Bible. In my experience, listening for God's voice does not mean expecting to hear an audible, Morgan Freeman-type voice from the sky. God's voice most often comes as a thought or stirring in my mind that aligns with His character, drawing me, in some way, to know Him, trust Him, and live out my faith.

While listening for the voice of God, you will inevitably come to the question, "Did God say that, or was that just in my own thoughts?" The first step in answering that question is, "Does the Bible have anything to say on this?" If it goes against something that the Bible says or against God's character and desires, then no, God did not say that. God will not say something that contradicts His Word. If the Bible affirms your thoughts or is silent on them, and what you heard is in line with God's character and desires, then it probably was from God. If you're still unsure, continue to seek God's guidance through more prayer and by inviting trusted believers to give you counsel.

We need to understand one more thing before we get into some of the specific practices of listening in prayer. You have to be willing to be "effectively ineffi-

> *In prayer. You have to be willing to be "effectively inefficient."*

cient." What I mean is this. We live in a fast-paced, "I want it now" society. When it comes to prayer, our impatience becomes ineffectively efficient—we blow through what we want to say, maybe read a few verses, and move on. This type of prayer is an efficient monologue but ineffective in that you're not communicating with God, giving time for Him to work on your heart and transform you. You may get a lot done in your "prayer time," but nothing transformative.

Effectively inefficient means you have to give space to listen and time for Him to speak. You have to slow down, to accomplish less in order to allow your thoughts and reading to lead you into a conversation with God. It's not efficient, but it will have a more significant effect on your spiritual life than if you speed through a lot of information, talk with God quickly, and move on.

I have personally found some of my richest prayer times while riding my bike for a few hours. I'll start by listening to an audio Bible. I then move into a time where I'm talking to God about my thankfulness and desires, and then I invite God to speak to me. Over the course of an hour or more, I may get distracted with random thoughts, but I don't fight them. Instead, I allow my thoughts to play themselves out in a conversation with God and find my way back to asking God to speak. I usually only have one or two things that God brings to my mind at random times in the ride. When He does, I ride on, intentionally focusing my thoughts on what has stirred in my mind and what it means for my relationship with Him and others. Sometimes only one thing pops into my head over a few hours. I don't get frustrated, expecting God to stream a constant flow of thoughts into my head. I give my mind space and time to hear things, and the extended time silences the lists of things I have to do which so often fill my head. It is not efficient, but it is way more effective than if I had just rushed through my prayers to get through them. Like a steak marinade, it takes time for the flavors to sink in, but the experience is so much more delicious by giving it the time it needs. Listening works best like a marinade—effectively inefficient.

With that said, here are a few ways you can practice listening in prayer:

1. <u>Be Quiet.</u>

Give yourself space and time, free from distractions, to sit, listen, and see if God brings anything to your mind. If you're anything like me, silence can be a bigger distraction than noise, as my thoughts clamor for attention. To solve this, you can turn on some worship music or go to a busy place with a bunch of white noise. You can also try to silence the thoughts in your head by meditatively focusing on God's characteristics. Each person's ability to be quiet and attentive to God is unique, so if you have a hard time being quiet, don't be discouraged. Keep trying to find places (beach, mountain, Starbucks, library) that allow you to listen for God's promptings. Even if you put all these things into practice, you may still have a hard time focusing, and you may not hear anything. Don't let that make you abandon this practice. Listening prayer is like a muscle; it must be exercised to gain strength. It may take you a while to get to a point where you don't get so distracted, and that is okay. The value of listening to God is worth the discipline it takes to get you there.

2. <u>Open Up The Bible With A Request For God To Speak.</u>

As I said before, listening prayer must have a firm foundation in God's Word. When you pray, ask God to speak to you through the reading of His Word. Then open up the Bible and start reading. Pay attention to what sticks out as odd, new, or challenging. Then stop and talk to God about those things. Don't rush on to read everything else. Sit with what God has drawn your attention to and ask yourself, "Why did God bring those things to my mind?" Allow this question to be the basis of your conversation with God. As you think through the answer, ask God to fill your thoughts with His and help you be obedient to His guidance.

3. Write Your Prayers.

Writing your prayers can significantly increase your focus and can help you realize what God is saying. Writing your prayers doesn't mean making a list of what you want God to do. It can include that, but it should involve opening up all your thoughts to God. Write down whatever God is bringing to your mind, where your heart is processing pain, joy, or struggle, any sin you need to confess, and any questions you have of Him.

One way to write your prayers is a free-flowing, spilling out of what is going on in your thoughts. With this type of 'writing your prayers,' don't try to make it structured—like you were taught in school. (God usually doesn't speak with a thesis statement and three supporting points.) Instead, give yourself permission to respond to what you are thinking through and pay attention to unique thoughts that reflect God's heart and Biblical truths. Here is an example:

God, as I struggle with finding deep friendships, you know how much this stinks, and I don't know what to do about it. I know your Word tells me that I'm valuable in your eyes, but I sometimes don't feel that. I hate that I just want to go to sleep when I get home from work, and I want to be filled with the joy you promised, but sometimes I don't feel that way. I want to be so overwhelmed by your love that this stuff doesn't hurt so bad. Remind me of my value in you. Just the other day, I was talking to Luke—thank you for him— and he told me about the trouble he is having at work. Would you give me wisdom as I support him in this challenging time? Today, when Greg came over to our house to talk, I just wanted him to go away. I'm not sure why he gets under my skin so much, but it seems like he's always complaining about something. I wonder how you would handle it. I really wish he wouldn't look to me for advice, but maybe there is something you want me to learn through him...Maybe there is some deeper issue going on, and he just wants to be loved or something like that. Well, God, help me love Greg as you do, and please help me find some good friendships...

As you can see, there isn't a pattern; it's just writing what is on your mind and using that to help you focus on what God might be saying. In the frustration with Greg, had I not written out a prayer, I wouldn't have slowed down enough to evaluate what God might be teaching me.

Another type of writing your prayers is more structured. Some people follow the pattern of the Lord's prayer which we looked at earlier. Some have a prayer book that gives prompts to pray through. The method I use starts with reading the Bible, then writing a quick synopsis of what I read and what stood out to me. I follow this by writing my prayer in a very free-flowing way and end by listing the things I need to do that day, as a way to ask God to guide me and give me wisdom in those things. Whatever method you use, know you're not stuck with that method and changing up approaches now and then can keep you from getting into a complacent pattern.

An added benefit of writing your prayers is the ability to look back and see where God has answered prayers, where you have grown, calling your attention to how He has moved in your life. Make sure that every once in a while you go back and re-read what you wrote in the past because it can help you see God's faithfulness and how He might be speaking to you now!

4. Write A Note From God To You.

The practice of writing a letter from God to yourself can be another beneficial way to hear God. Start this practice by asking God to guide the pen as you write His thoughts. This is not a "Bible Ouija board," promising a direct revelation from God. Writing the note should be Biblically accurate and faithful to God's character. Yes, it will involve your thoughts, but by taking God's perspective, you're forced to try to think about His thoughts (listening). Since prayer is a dialogue, begin by writing a short letter to God about what you want His guidance on, your struggles, what you're thankful for, and whatever else comes to your mind. Then start penning the letter in response from God to you. Think through your writing with what you know the Bible says and what you think God would say, and make it personal. Don't just quote Bible verses; write a letter. If there are verses to quote, expand on them as a father would do to his children.

For example:

Don't Do: *Drew, you said you're lonely, remember, "God loved the world so much that He gave His only son!" So, God loves you... I hope this helps.*

Do: *Drew, you said you're lonely, and I'm so sorry you feel that way. I know the pain and the hurt of loneliness is crushing. My heart breaks that the enemy has stirred this darkness because I want you to remember, "God loved the world so much that He gave His only son!" Even if everyone else abandons you, I will not. I will not. I will not. I love you, and I thought of you on the cross. I know your heartache, and I am working on it. It may not be the timing you want but trust me.*

When I've written a letter from God to me, it has allowed a depth of communication and experience which I was not expecting. Even as I wrote the example statement, I was drawn to the love of God in a fresh way. Because this approach can give God a more tangible voice, it may also expose you to a conversation with God you never expected.

This happened for me, in a life-altering way, between 11th and 12th grade. My high school years could be defined by the statement, "I want a girlfriend." While there were a few months in those years where I had a girlfriend, most of my time was spent in a desperate pursuit of girls. Even though I had been highly unsuccessful in having a girlfriend in my first three years of high school, my senior year would be different. With a new look and a growth spurt that helped me look older than a ten year old, I was going to live out my *Saved by the Bell*-Zach Morris-Kelly Kapowski dream. (*Saved by the Bell* was a fantastic '90s show... well, maybe just a 90's show).

Before my senior year, I attended a church service where the pastor gave everyone time to reflect, pray, and write themselves a note from God. He directed us to focus on what God might be calling us to do in the next year. I began the letter, writing out my thoughts (which, of course, included wanting a girlfriend). Then, as I wrote God's response to me, I was shocked to see words forming in my mind and on the page, calling me to give up my pursuit of girls to focus on my relationship with God. This was definitely from God because it absolutely wasn't from me.

During my senior year, I was far from perfect in keeping my focus on God. Still, the note did shift my perspective from a consumed, incessant pursuit of girls. This made my senior year way more enjoyable. It allowed me to have friendships with girls without the obnoxiousness of me hoping there would be "more to our relationship." That freedom helped me ask a girl to prom that would "never date Drew," ... and now that girl is my wife!!!

Fear And Eloquence

Before we conclude this section, one more thing needs to be said. For many people praying (especially out loud) is hugely intimidating and brings great fear. I know a few sen-

> *The key to prayer is a reverent heart, not eloquent speech.*

tences probably won't wipe away your fear, but I'll try. The key to prayer is a reverent heart, not eloquent speech. Many people get overwhelmed with not wanting to sound stupid. That concern reveals a heart more oriented to what others think, rather than what God thinks. Remember, God already knows your heart. He already knows you. He already loves you. Praying is just affirming what He already knows, expressing faith in Him. If you are so worried about what others think as you pray, perhaps your focus is wrong.

On top of that, if you are praying and people are judging you, then I encourage you to dismiss their judgement. You are speaking to God, not to them. They have no right to rob you of an opportunity to continue developing your relationship with Him.

Lastly, your vulnerable, unsure prayer might be the very thing God is calling you to express. Your fumbled words may actually encourage and help others in their prayers. You might be an infant in your prayer life, but there could be someone who has a "baby faith" and needs your bravery to show them how to begin. When fear is trying to silence you from praying, remember Romans 8:26-27: "And the Holy Spirit helps us in our weakness. For example, we don't know what God wants us to pray for. But the Holy Spirit prays for us with groanings that cannot be expressed in words. And the Father who knows all hearts knows what the Spirit is saying, for the Spirit pleads for us believers in harmony with God's own will."

How cool is that? You can talk to God without worrying about messing up the words or being eloquent because the Holy Spirit is interceding for you. As you speak to God, you should have a deep reverence for Him as well as a thankful heart that He has made Himself available to talk to—and forget about what others think of you.

Remember, God wants to communicate with you. He doesn't desire for your prayer life to be tedious drudgery. By practicing these different ways to engage in prayer, your prayer life can have times of vibrant connection with the Creator. Prayer is still a discipline. You shouldn't expect that once you try a new prayer style your connection with God will be forever engaging, but these techniques will remind you to not buy into the lie that prayer is a one-way monologue to a God far away. God is in you. He is with you. He loves you. He wants to talk with you. When you give yourself space to listen to God and respond to what He says, it will change your life. Prayer allows your relationship with God to deepen and your effectiveness for Him to increase... so, pray always.

> *You can talk to God without worrying about messing up the words or being eloquent because the Holy Spirit is interceding for you.*

Questions For Reflection:

- What is the most challenging part of praying for you?

- Have you ever had an especially good prayer time? Describe the circumstances that helped lead to that.

- What about "the Lord's Prayer" as a pattern, stood out to you the most? Why?

- Which of the listening practices have you tried? How was that experience?

- Who is someone you know that loves to pray?

- Ask them what they do to foster a passion for prayer and write down what you learned.

Chapter 11

Meditation

"They delight in the law of the Lord, meditating on it day and night" (Psalm 1:2).

"I lie awake thinking of you, meditating on you through the night" (Psalm 63:6).

Meditation: imagine, mourn, mutter, roar, speak, study, talk, utter.[1] To think intently and at length, as for spiritual purposes. To reflect deeply on a subject.[2]

Meditation is a confusing word in our society. For many, it stirs up images of sitting cross-legged, humming something with eyes rolled to the back of your head. This view of meditation has its roots in eastern religions. The purpose is to clear one's mind from the chaos and distractions of life, with the end goal being a state of mind free from all thoughts.

The Christian discipline of meditation is drastically different in that it aims to clear the mind of worldly distractions to be filled with God's truth. The end goal is not an empty mind, but a mind filled with the things of God. In Christian meditation, you are invited to intently fix your mind on God. Unfortunately, this extremely valuable practice is too often dismissed with the busyness of life. Many people speed through their time with God, gleaning the easy truth or application. Meditation slows you down to soak in God's presence, to absorb His Word. It gives space for God's Truth to root itself in your soul. To meditate properly, you must not simply want to retain more knowledge of God; you must desire to know God more. Correct Christian meditation will also affect your life outside of the specific moment of meditation. Morton Kelsey explains: "Christian meditation that does not make a difference in the quality of one's outer life is short-circuited. It may flare for a while, but unless it results in finding richer and more loving relationships with other human beings, or in changing conditions in the world that cause human suffering, the chances are that an individual's prayer activity will fizzle out."[3]

> *The end goal is not an empty mind, but a mind filled with the things of God*

Focusing Intently On God Has To Draw You Closer To His Heart

Recently I performed a wedding in which the maid of honor was the bride's sister who had moved from the United States to England two years prior. As she started her maid-of-honor speech, my wife turned to me in shock, asking if the person speaking was the bride's sister. The reason for the surprise was that the maid of honor spoke with a British accent. After two years of being surrounded by the Brits' cheery intonations, she had been influenced to talk like them. I'm sure she didn't intend to change the way she sounded, but the effect of being in England made her sound British. This is the same with meditation with God: You can't spend intense time with Him without picking up His mannerisms and starting to sound and act like Him. The importance of this cannot be missed.

If you spend time genuinely meditating on God and His Word, you will change. Get ready for it. On the other hand, if you are meditating on God and no change is produced, you need to evaluate what other things in your life may be fighting against the change. If you meditate, then go to work where you lie, cheat, and steal, or go into your living room where you mistreat your spouse, then perhaps your meditation is more of a self-satisfying religious accomplishment and not proper meditation. Proper meditation is eager for God to make you more like Him.

How Then Do We Meditate?

In his book *Celebration of Discipline*, Richard Foster says, "We learn to meditate by meditating."[4] Meditation is something that we must commit to and practice. A meaningful life of meditation takes discipline.

> *Proper meditation is eager for God to make you more like Him.*

For many, this starts with scheduling time to meditate, ensuring the busyness of life does not crowd it out. Meditation is so vital that every full-time staff member at our church is given one paid "day away" per month to pray and meditate. Even though we provide this time, if I don't put it on my calendar and keep it sacred, the "have-to-dos" will squeeze it out. I know it is rare to have a work that requires you to spend time with God, but the value of making sure you have regular opportunities to meditate shouldn't be abandoned because of inconvenience. After you've scheduled the time, here are some suggestions to make the most of your meditation.

Preparing Your Body And Mind

Meditation can happen anywhere but finding a location with as few distractions as possible is best. This means turning off your cell phone. Don't just put it on silent, because you know the devil will have all your friends texting like never before to distract you from this opportunity. As you enter into a distraction-free zone, the real work begins as you prepare your heart and mind to intensely focus on God.

Close your eyes and ask God to clear your mind of distractions so your attention can be solely on Him. Open your Bible, listen to a worship song, or find another way to focus your mind on Him. If you get distracted, repeat your prayer, asking God to help you focus on Him. You may have to repeat your request many times in your head or out loud.

As you start, don't be discouraged by an easily distracted mind. Instead, when your mind drifts to something you need to do or remember, write it down, and move back to focusing on God. If the distraction is a random thought that doesn't need to be written down, gently guide your mind back to God. It usually isn't helpful to think "stop thinking that" because "stop thinking that" usually produces more thoughts on the very thing you don't want to think about. "Gently" means allowing the idea to exist while using it to draw you back to your conversation with God. Here is an example: "Why is that bird circling over there? I bet it's looking for prey. I wonder if it's going to dive down and grab something. It's pretty crazy that God gives birds the vision to see that far off... I wonder if there is anything in my life that God wants me to see that I'm ignoring."

Some people have named this type of processing a "Jesus juke." Basically, it means bringing up "God" in a situation that doesn't seem to fit. But here's the thing: if you've entered into a time of meditation to hear from God, maybe the distraction of the bird was what He was using to get you to hear from Him. If anything, the question you ended up asking is still a good one to meditate on. If you're still having a hard time meditating because of mental distractions, it may help to exhale those distracting thoughts. Simply breathe out "bird" (or whatever it is that is distracting you) as a prayer to release the distraction to God. Another suggestion is to use white noise, or some sort of music, to help you focus your mind. These are just a couple of suggestions to eliminate the mind noise. If they don't work, continue to explore other ways to help you move to a focused meditation on God.

Preparing Your Heart

After you find a space that will allow you to focus, you must prepare your heart, inviting God to fill your mind with His thoughts. This can be a short request that moves you to the next step or can be a repetitive request that helps focus your mind on Him. Keep this time simple. There is no need to find a bunch of different ways to say the same thing. God knows what you desire, and your attention should be on God, not your words. Remember that approaching God with a repetitive request is not to be done like a child who nags his mother for something until he gets it. The repetition is intended to sink deeper into the desire to meet with God and be transformed by Him.

As you do this, think about what you are asking Him to do. Attune your heart to Him. Relax. Allow His thoughts to stir in your mind. If something comes to your head, focus on it. Ask God why that thought came to your mind. Explore your heart to see if there is something God wants you to do with that thought. When you think you have your answers to those questions, dig deeper. Sit with them longer and allow God more time to speak.

Too often, we want a list from God of what He wants us to do or how He is going to grow us so we can quickly check it off. That is not what meditation is about. Digging deeper means sitting with your thoughts longer to explore what they mean for your interaction with God. Ask God questions about yourself, about Him, about what He wants. Ask Him to continue to challenge and encourage you with what He is bringing to your mind. Stay attentive to His voice, praying that the things He is communicating will soak into your soul. Meditation is not a discipline where you are trying to get a lot done. It is instead about having a narrow, intense focus, allowing His love and truth to personally address you and sink into your heart.

> *Digging deeper means sitting with your thoughts longer to explore what they mean for your interaction with God.*

The previous steps may be all that you need to meditate; however, the open-endedness may still be difficult and distracting for some. So, you can do a few other things during your meditation to help focus your time with God.

Thankfulness

Take time to draw your mind to things for which you are thankful. "Every good and perfect gift is from above, coming down from the Father of the heavenly lights" (Js. 1:7, NIV). If every good and perfect gift is from God, you should regularly thank Him for those things. Centering your mind on thanksgiving acknowledges God's lordship and love and puts your heart in a posture of reverence. Meditating on your thankfulness for God's expressions of love is an easy way to start your meditation since God's blessings are all around. Your life. Your friends. Your church. Your family. The food you ate this morning. The warmth of the sun. Meditating on the broader things I just mentioned is a good reminder that everything is a gift from God, but don't stop there. Try to think as specific and personal as possible. (Like an interaction you had with a friend last weekend, or your love and ability to do _____.)

While meditating on thanksgiving, don't rush through the list. Pause. Ponder what you are thanking God for. Think about the fact that God has gifted you each good thing. Push yourself to be thankful for detailed things, not just general. If you're thankful for your job think more specifically about what it is you like about your job. (The ability to problem-solve, your co-workers, the window in your office, sitting by the copier and smelling the freshly printed paper... etc.) As you discover more things you are thankful for, meditate on what each gift says about God's character and His love for you.

Verses

God's Word should always be the underpinning of your meditation, but this meditative method centers around a repeated reflection on a small set of verses. Like correct Bible study, read verses within context, making sure you understand what the author means. Unlike Bible study, the primary goal is not to examine the text but to reflectively allow the verses to draw you to God's thoughts and allow them to examine you. Dietrich Bonhoeffer explains,"...just as you do not analyze the words of someone you love, but accept them as they are said to you, accept the Word of Scripture and ponder it in your heart, as Mary did. That is all. That is meditation."[5]

> *Notice anything that sticks out, anything to which God might be drawing your attention.*

As you read, notice anything that sticks out, anything to which God might be drawing your attention. If you have something come to your mind, focus on why God might have drawn your thoughts to that idea, and mull over whatever has been stirred. Repeat the verse over and over out loud or in your thoughts. Meditating by exploring what God is saying to you or about you in that verse. If you read a section of the Bible and nothing sticks out, don't move on. Re-read the passage again and again, inviting God to bring new things to your mind as you read.

When an idea pops into your head, allow it to linger, reflecting on God's character and your interaction with Him. Sometimes your thoughts will clearly correlate with what you're reading. Occasionally God will use the reading to stir something in your heart that doesn't have to do with the text but draws you to Him nonetheless. If evil thoughts come to your mind, pray against them, and ask Jesus to fill your thoughts with His. If God-honoring thoughts come to your mind, pause and meditate on why God brought those to your mind, asking Him what He wants you to know or do. After you have meditated on these things, read and re-read the verses again to see if there is anything else God wants you to meditate on.

Imagination

When is the last time you "used your imagination"? As a kid, I'm sure there were plenty of times when an adult encouraged you to do this. Ironically, as we get older, the very value we encourage is something we use less and less frequently. This is too bad because engaging your imagination can be just as valuable as an adult as when you were a child, especially when it comes to meditation.

Imagination invites you to explore your Bible reading and thoughts less like a college course and more like a fantasy movie. Using your imagination can help you experience God in new ways by moving you from a reader of God's Word to a participator in God's Word. Imagination breaks up the routine of textbook-like reading by slowing you down while you imaginatively use all five senses to enter into the story. As you imagine what you are reading, think about the sounds, smells, colors, textures, tastes, and invite God to help you notice what He wants you to focus on.

Imagination can also help you engage your thoughts in a more meaningful, meditative way. When thoughts, convictions, or feelings enter your mind, don't analyze them; use your imagination to give them images and stories.

Imagining your thoughts might look like this: if you've been in emotional turmoil give your pain an image. What does it feel like the pain is doing? Perhaps your pain becomes a weighty backpack, pulling you down. Then your imagination has you on a journey in a dark forest, with the burden of a backpack dragging you to a halt, hindering you from moving on. Through the dense trees, you hear a powerful yet caring voice that says, "keep going." Although you can't see where the voice came from, you immediately know it is God's. So, with muscles aching, you continue your difficult journey. The forest soon turns to a desert, and your hike turns into hours of marching through sweltering sand. Just when you are about to give up, you see an oasis, and as you approach the shade and water, you sense a mighty presence behind you.

Once again, you know it is God. He walks up behind you, surprising you with the ease in which He gently lifts the backpack off your weary shoulders. He then places the backpack in front of you, and with loving eyes, looks at you before beginning to open it. As He starts unzipping the top, darkness like you've never seen before sucks in the light surrounding the opening of the backpack. God then reaches into the void, and you see Him wince. As wince that you know is causing much more pain than He is letting on. A moment later, the darkness explodes to light, and what he pulls from the backpack shocks your breath away. At the same time your lungs are trying to regain their composure and suck in much-needed air, your heart begins to hurt-but the hurt is good, deep, and profound. What you see changes everything.

In His hand, where the nails of the cross have left a void, are words that represent your worst secrets and pains. To your continued amazement, those words, in His hands, are being absorbed in His palms, in His light, in His love.

This exercise in imagination could go on and on, but I'll stop there to allow God to fill your thoughts with His thoughts. Before, during, and after, make sure you ask God to direct your imagination to what He wants. After you've journeyed through your imaginative experience, take time to further meditate on what God revealed to you.

A last reminder: Meditation takes practice and patience. Start small. Set aside 5-10 minutes a few times a month and give yourself time to learn and grow.

Questions For Reflection:

- Have you ever practiced Christian meditation? If you have, how was the experience for you? If you haven't, why not?

- What do you think would be the toughest thing about meditation?

- What do you think would be the greatest benefit of meditation?

- What are you thankful for?

- As you reflect on your thankfulness, did anything come to your mind that surprised you?

- Do you think using your imagination will be easy or difficult for you? Why?

- What do you think imagination could do to enhance your interaction with God?

- What might God be showing you about Himself as you practice this discipline?

- What might He be trying to show you about yourself?

- Practice meditation this week and write about the experience.

Chapter 12

Confession

A few days ago, I looked up a musician I've heard a lot about, unfamiliar with his music but wanting to see if it was something I'd like. I clicked on the first music video suggested and found the song entertaining and catchy. I listened to lyrics carefully to make sure there wasn't anything vulgar. To my delight, it all sounded great. But one song is not a big enough sample size to confirm cleanliness and artistry.

I clicked on the next music video and again listened to a catchy song with decent lyrics. I clicked on the next video, and a "parental warning" appeared. Not taking the warning as a clue to discontinue watching, I allowed the video to play. The opening scene was a little gory, and I could kind of see why it had the advisory. A few more seconds into the video, the obviousness of why there was a parental advisory warning became apparent. Instead of turning it off, I jumped to a later part of the video, trying to skip over the inappropriate part. Once again, the images were crude, and once again, instead of turning it off, I tried to skip to another part of the song. And again, the same thing, this time with slight hesitation as I finally decided to turn it off.

Immediately following this instance, the Spirit convicted me of not shutting off the video right away. His conviction also prompted me to confess this to my wife. The struggle was real. I justified not confessing with: "I didn't mean to." "I skipped ahead." "I didn't watch the whole thing." "She doesn't need to know." "It's not that big of a deal." All these reasons not to confess were in direct opposition to the Holy Spirit. They were strategies of the devil to keep me away from the benefits of confession. With all those excuses still clawing at my mind, God gave me the strength to confess to my wife. I apologized and found peace in her forgiveness and a weakening of sin's power over me.

Correcting Misunderstandings Of Confession

To confess (v.)—to admit to a punishable deed or sin.[1]

Depending on your background, the idea of confession may make you cringe. After all, confession makes you reflect on how messed up you are and may feel like excessive wallowing in your sins. Our culture says, "failures show weakness" and "confession is just the church's way to control you." Because of these flawed understandings of confession, it may be something you've tried to steer clear of. The problem with these worldly perspectives is two-fold.

First, your initial act of faith in Christ is confessional. Accepting Jesus as your sacrificed and risen Savior begins by admitting that you need a Savior because you have sin in your life that you cannot make up for. First John 1:9 says, "If we confess our sins,

He is faithful and just to forgive us our sins and to cleanse us from all unrighteousness." Without confession, there remains a relational gap between you and God. By confessing your sins, you accept the work Jesus has done on your behalf to bring you into a right relationship with God, but this verse is not only about future salvation. John is writing to Christians. The confession he is calling them to engage in is a regular practice for continuing sanctification. In other words, as you confess your sins, you bring them to the light, and God works to move you from them.

Second, maybe you come from a tradition that used your confession to control you. Perhaps you've been made to think that God wants you to confess so He can use guilt to get you to do His bidding. This is not the Biblical view of confession. Truly repentant confession should bring healing and freedom.

Psalm 103:12 proclaims, "He has removed our sins as far from us as the east is from the west." God's love takes your confession and places the weight of that sin on His son, Jesus, who has already

> *"He has removed our sins as far from us as the east is from the west." Psalm 103:12*

received the due penalty. Jesus' act on the cross is finished, complete, and your sins have been paid for. Christ's sacrifice makes it so that confession should be somberly joyful. As you confess your sins, your heart should regret what you have done with a desire remove it from your life. You should be sorrowful because your sin hurts God, others, and was a reason for Jesus' suffering on the cross. BUT confession should also draw you to a deep joy because you are admitting your sins to the God who has already done the work to make you right with Him. You should be joyful that "while you were still a sinner Christ died for you" (Romans 5:8).

The fact that Jesus' work is finished, the payment for your sin is complete, and He rose from the dead, should fill you with gratitude and praise. In a complete reversal of culture's understanding, confession provides the way to move on to true freedom. Remember, God is not sitting in heaven impatiently tapping His foot, rolling His eyes with frustration, waiting for you to "just confess." I believe a more accurate picture is one where God is sitting next to you, His arm around you, lovingly begging you to see that your sin is harming you and others. As you sit together, He reminds you of the hard work He has already done. He shows you He is the answer to your issues and asks you to allow Him to help you avoid that sin in the future. Confession is an invitation from God to trust Him with all your issues and let Him move you from them.

True Confession

True Christian confession is admitting your sin with repentance. Repentance is a regretful remorse with a desire to remove the sin. Christian confession is unlike our legal system, where someone can confess to a crime with no remorse. "Yeah, I did it, so what?" is technically a confession, but it isn't the type of confession we're talking about here. This does not mean that the discipline of confession has to be laced with tears and desperate pleas for forgiveness. It does mean that if you're approaching God just to get stuff off your chest, you're missing the point of confession. Again, true Christian confession is admitting your sin with repentance.

> *True Christian confession is admitting your sin with repentance. Repentance is a regretful remorse with a desire to remove the sin.*

How To Confess

Now that you know what confession is and how to approach it, start your confession by asking the Holy Spirit to reveal the sins in your life. Think through all your actions and attitudes. This may mean replaying the day in your mind to see where sin arose. It may be best to continue to repeat "reveal my sin" until something comes to mind. As things pop into your head, avoid the temptation to justify them. If the Spirit has brought it to your mind, don't fight it. Realize God has already paid the price, and confess your sins.

The more specific you can be about the actions and attitudes that were sinful, the better. The late author and Christian leader Watchman Nee explains, "Children of God should not make a general confession by acknowledging their innumerable sins in a vague manner, because such confession does not provide conscience opportunity to do its (Holy Spirit's) perfect work. They ought to allow the Holy Spirit through their conscience to point out their sins one by one. Christians must accept its reproach and be willing, according to the mind of the Spirit, to eliminate everything which is contrary to God."[2] Being general in your confession is like a football coach who tells his players to "get better" without looking specifically at what they need to do. Is the coach offering good advice? Yes, the team should always strive to get better. Is it really that helpful, though? Not really. It would be more useful if the coach sat down with each player, evaluating every play and pointing out where corrections need to be made—confession functions in the same way. The process of being specific takes

> *Being general in your confession is like a football coach who tells his players to "get better" without looking specifically at what they need to do.*

more time and is more painful, but the opportunity to grow is so much greater.

Again, God has already forgiven you, but the repentant confession is a healthy remembrance of the need for His forgiveness. Once you've acknowledged the sin and asked for forgiveness, enter back into allowing the Spirit to bring other sins to your mind. Repeat this process until you can think of nothing else. Don't rush this. Asking the Spirit to search the depth of your heart and mind, and giving Him space to do so, will be tough but will bring greater freedom as you confess deeper issues. End your time of confession with thanksgiving for the truth that He loves you so much that He gave His Son, Jesus, to die for you. Thank Jesus for His conquering work which allows you to be in a relationship with Him despite everything you just confessed.

Continued Confession

The next step of confession is very, very difficult but crucial. It can be the catalyst for the transformation God wants to produce in your life. See, it's one thing to confess your sins to God, but if your sin has harmed someone else, you may have a responsibility to confess to them as well. Here's why: your relationship with God should affect your relationship with others, and your relationship with others affects your relationship with God. Confessing to God without taking steps to confess to those you've offended falls short of the opportunity to grow in your Christ-likeness.

My four children sometimes do things to hurt or annoy one another, resulting in some sort of punishment. When their time-out or other punishment is over, my wife or I talk to them about the wrong they've done, and most times, they respond to us with a "sorry." While we are thankful for this response, there is another confession that they need to make to set things right. They need to apologize to the sibling they offended. If they refuse to apologize, they go back on time-out until they are ready to do so. I'm not saying that God is going to sit you on time-out until you make amends for all your sins. What I am saying is if you are sincerely confessing with repentance your confession should also be offered to the person you offended.

Now, not all your confession will be something you bring to others. If you find yourself lusting or thinking negative thoughts about someone, you may not need to let them know your sinful desires. In cases like this, confession to others is still really important, but instead of confessing to the person you are thinking about, you should confess to a trusted friend who will help you move to more Christ-like thoughts and actions. As difficult as it is to confess how corrupt your mind is, and as much as your heart is telling you to be quiet, confessing to someone else brings the sin to light and lessens its power. You will also bring awareness to your sin so the person to whom you are confessing can hold you accountable to moving from it.

It's counterintuitive. Your heart will tell you confession makes you weak, broken, and foolish, when the exact opposite is true. Confession takes strength, allows God to put the brokenness together, and wisely exposes the sin to help you root it out of your life.

Not Offloading

When confessing your sins, you need to be careful to not allow it to become an exercise of just offloading guilt without ever actually dealing with your sin. God doesn't want you to dwell on your sins once confessed. You've been forgiven. But too often, I've seen confession as an excuse to never do the hard work of removing, and turning from, the confessed sin.

I have met with a lot of guys who struggle with looking at pornography. When they confess their sin, I praise them for their willingness to share with me and pray with them to overcome. We often talk about steps they need to take to eliminate the opportunities for temptation, and I urge them to rely on God for strength. I'll then set up another time to meet and check in with them. The good news is a lot of the guys I've met have responded well to this structure. Even though the struggle continues and at times they fail, they take the steps we talked about.

The bad news is many guys confess the same sin every week without taking any action to remove it from their lives. Their confession has them walking out of a meeting, feeling better about themselves because they've confessed, but their sense of relief is not from a heart of true repentant confession. Their sense of relief is because their guilt has been offloaded. In some of the conversations, I've realized the only reason they are confessing and "feel bad" is because they have to share that they screwed up again. In other words, they aren't sorry for the sin; they're sorry for having to talk about the sin.

True confession involves repentance, and true repentance involves actions that align with that repentance. This does not mean if you confess a sin and sin again you haven't really confessed. It merely means that as you confess make sure that your

> *As you confess make sure that your heart desires to turn from the sin and toward Christ-likeness.*

heart desires to turn from the sin and toward Christ-likeness. Proper confession should lead to living differently. When you confess to someone, feel the shame of the sin, realize the love and forgiveness of Christ, and allow His love to be the strength and motivation to make the changes needed.

The Enemy Of Confession

The biggest enemy of confession is pride. Pride will tell you that "they deserved it," "you don't need to worry about it," "it's just not that big of a deal," and even "I'm trying to spare them."

"They deserved it," makes them responsible for your actions. From a worldly point of view, perhaps they did deserve it, but from a godly point of view, your response to others should be motivated to show them Christ's love. Pride tries to convince you that you don't need to humble yourself and confess because you're justified in your sin.

"You don't need to worry about it," and "it's just not that big of a deal" minimize sin. These statements basically say, "God, you're getting too worked up over something you shouldn't." Confession says, "I understand the gravity of sin, and I want to get as far from it as possible."

All these excuses tend to find their way to the final statement that seems so loving but is, once again, prideful: "I'm trying to spare them." Here, your pride is trying to persuade you to disobey God's Word for the sake of relational harmony. James 5:16 says, "Confess your sins to each other and pray for each other so that you may be healed…" God's motivation for confession is relational harmony for the sake of His Kingdom. God knows the path to this is exposing our brokenness to one another so we can move forward, together, with Him. By refusing to confess to others, your sin stays hidden and a relational divide remains. Is confession to others difficult? Absolutely, but when you confess, it allows your sin to be exposed, your relationship to move on in truth, and healing to truly begin.

One more thing to help process your interaction with the Holy Spirit when it comes to confession. Pay attention to any reactions that sound like one of the excuses we just talked about. These excuses tend to be a direct reaction to a prompting the Holy Spirit has given you to move to confession. This means that if you sense any of these excuses swirl in your head, it's a good indication that you need to do the opposite, and you need to confess. As tough as it is, remember, Jesus called us to lay down our lives and serve others. Look to Christ and the example He set, loving you and pursuing you, even though you don't deserve it. If you call yourself a Christ-follower, you shouldn't allow these excuses to stop you from the opportunity to show great humility and love by repentantly confessing your sins.

Questions For Reflection:

- What were your thoughts when reading about confession?

- What was your background or understanding of confession before reading this?

- How has your perspective changed after reading this?

- What do you think about the idea of "eagerly entering into confession"?

- Do you have someone you trust with your confessions?

- Explain the difference between confession and truly repentant confession (true confession).

Chapter 13

Fasting

"I'm soooooo hungry."

"You just ate an hour ago."

"Yeah, but I feel like I could die."

"You said you were, 'so stuffed you could die,' after dinner."

"Ahhhhhhhhhhhh!" (falling on the ground in eye-rolling agony)

If you've ever been around a child, this is a conversation you may have heard many times. My wife homeschools our children, and the number of times my kids say, "I'm so hungry," is quite high (don't worry, we feed our kids properly). Food is obviously important as it gives you the strength and energy to live, but I'd argue it's not as important as you think. Often, if my wife or I can redirect the kid's attention to another activity, the "starvation" magically goes away. In the same way, turning your hunger pangs into reminders to focus on God can minimize your hunger and has enormous spiritual value. Fasting is a way to help you realize the nutrients food provides is not nearly as important as the nutrients God provides.

Unfortunately, many people believe fasting is for the religiously extreme, the 'super Christians.' The thought of not eating for a day, a week, or a month is dismissed because, "There is just no way I could survive." Fasting is equated to nothing more than a way to build the muscle of suffering, and surely life will provide that in other ways, so why put yourself in that situation? Many of the reasons people don't fast (except for medical reasons) reveal a significant undervaluation of the wonderful things fasting does for your relationship with God. These excuses tend to come from a poor understanding of this transformational discipline.

Sadly, unless your perspective of fasting changes, you probably won't ever experience the unique and profound interactions you can have with God through fasting. So, let me take some time to help you see what fasting is and its benefits.

What Is Fasting?

Fasting is so much more than not eating. It is a practice that can be enormously transformational when engaged in with the right heart. I'll share my fasting experiences with you, but let's first look at what Jesus says in Matthew 6:16-18:

"And when you fast, don't make it obvious, as the hypocrites do, for they try to look miserable and disheveled so people will admire them for their fasting. I tell you the truth, that is the only reward they will ever get. But when you fast, comb your hair and wash your face. Then no one will notice that you are fasting, except your Father, who knows what you do in private. And your Father, who sees everything, will reward you."

The first thing to notice is Jesus' assumption that His followers will be fasting. Jesus doesn't say, "and, if you decide to fast..." He says, "...and, WHEN you fast." Jesus knows the importance of fasting and believes that those who follow Him will participate in this discipline.

Second, Jesus clearly teaches that fasting should be done without drawing attention to yourself, but this doesn't mean that you never talk about

> *Jesus assumes His followers will fast.*

it. There is a way to share your fasting experience that honors God and encourages others to participate in this fantastic discipline. You definitely need to be careful when you talk about fasting since it can quickly become a prideful boast, but complete silence on this discipline can eliminate the opportunity to glorify God and show others that fasting is something everyone can and should do. I first considered this discipline because one of my mentors, without bragging, would talk openly about his experiences and methods of fasting.

Mindset Of Fasting

With that said, I've fasted in a few different ways that have each had their difficulties, but each has been well worth it. One year I fasted from fast-food—one year from soda. I've done a liquid-only fast a few times, and I've fasted from non-food elements. A couple of these fasts focused on a specific issue for which I was seeking God's guidance. A few have been to remind myself that God should be my primary "want."

In each fast, I learned things about God and myself that I would have had a much harder time learning had I not removed food (or another element) from my life. There were

> *The benefits of fasting significantly outweigh whatever discomfort you'll feel.*

days where it was miserable, but every time I've found the benefits significantly outweigh whatever discomfort I felt. In fact, the pain and desires were great tools God used to draw my attention to Him during the fasts. When it comes to fasting from food, I've learned when you are extremely hungry, your mind tells you food is a lot better than it actually is.

Don't get me wrong, I LOVE FOOD, but when you haven't eaten in weeks, you begin to think a steak or cake is going to be the most marvelous thing ever. When you break your fast and eat those things you've been craving, you realize that, while it is good, it only satisfies for such a short time. This is one of the bonuses of fasting—truly experiencing Jesus' words, "Man shall live on bread alone, but by every word that comes from the mouth of God." (Mt. 4:4, NIV) In other words:

Food = momentarily delicious and sustaining.

God's Word = eternally delicious and sustaining.

Again, every fast has elements of struggle and frustration. Still, the beauty of a fast is that God takes those difficulties and molds them into a richer hunger and love for Him.

How To Fast- Not Just Remove...Replace.

Fasting must start with a direction. The overarching direction of a Christian fast will always be about giving up something important to you (food, entertainment, shopping, etc.) to focus on something essential (God). Fasts tell your body and your soul, "God is more important than my cravings, and I want to discipline my physical needs (and wants) to focus on my spiritual needs." Having a direction in your fast is so important because, without it, your decision to fast from something isn't fasting—it's just starving yourself of that activity. Your focus should be answered by these questions: "What do I want out of this?" or "Why am I fasting?"

Although you can have multiple focuses for your fast, and at times more than one thing is revealed during your fast, it is best to narrow your focus as much as possible. If your focus is too broad, it is easy to get distracted and not dive deep into that thing you're fasting for. Using

> *"God is more important than my cravings, and I want to discipline my physical needs to focus on my spiritual needs."*

your fast to ponder, reflect, plead, and seek God will allow your thoughts to be refined and your interaction with Him to be richer.

The focus of fasting can be either inward or outward. An *inward approach* focuses on aligning your heart and mind with God's. Here are just a few inward focuses you can have during your fast:

- A deeper understanding of God or yourself.

- An increased desire to follow God and His Word.

- Dealing with the root of a sin issue.

- An awareness of your inability to earn God's love, replaced with a better understanding of God's overwhelming love for you.

- An aspect of God's character that you want to grasp better.

Although an inward-directed fast focuses less on an action you need to take, any inward revelation and realization should produce outward change.

An *outward-focused* fast is goal-oriented and is actionable. It's about aligning your hands and feet with God's. Some of the outward focuses of fasting are:

- Removal of a vice.

- Spending less time on mindless activities and more time on Kingdom-building activities.

- Opportunities to talk to a friend about salvation.

- Discipline to fight sin.

- The direction of your life.

- Healing of a relationship.

- Seeking an answer to a prayer.

Whether you have an inward or outward focus, make sure you have a focus to guide your motivation and your mind during the fast.

Once you have your focus, determine the length and type of fast you will embark on. I recommend starting with something slightly more difficult than you're comfortable with. I've found that beginning "easy" doesn't give your soul the space it needs to really long for what you are seeking. This is not a hard and fast rule by any means. Some fasting is better than no fasting. Still, a 24-hour fast is usually just long enough to be uncomfortable, but not long enough to allow your discomfort to be the motivation for diving deeper into your direction.

I've had a few experiences where the first one to three days were almost a waste of time without days four through the end. The first few days I was more focused on what I wasn't eating, and it wasn't until the later days that I thought to myself, "I don't want to just 'not eat,' I want this to be so much more than that."

It took a few days to help me see this, prompting me to invest my body, mind, and soul into drawing the most out of the fast. You may be different and starting with a 24- or 48-hour fast is well beyond anything you ever thought. If that's you, great! Start small and see how it goes. Next time you fast, see if you can go longer to develop your focus even more. Remember, a fast isn't for comfort and ease, so if you get to a place where you say, "This is just too hard," don't give up. Ask God for strength to continue. Learning to be desperate for God's power and presence will hugely benefit you.

Decide what type of fast it will be. There are many ways to fast: food, TV, sports, social media, music, and more. Fasting from food is the most common and can be done in several ways: liquid or water only, a removal of a type of food, one meal a day, etc. Whichever fast you go with, make sure you eliminate something that consumes a significant part of your life. You want to feel the loss of it, to experience the value and gain of time with God. Choosing something you don't care about or rarely consume will be less effective in reminding you of what you've given up. The pain of what you've removed is one of the most important elements of the fast because it draws you to a more desperate and regular engagement with God.

> *If you get to a place where you say, "This is just too hard," don't give up. Ask God for strength to continue. Learning to be desperate for God's power and presence will significantly benefit you.*

Don't Do it Alone

After you've determined your fast length and focus, either ask a friend to fast with you or ask them to pray with you and encourage you throughout your fast. This will help you process what God is doing during your fast and stay accountable to it. Removing something important from your life is difficult, so having someone hold you accountable, especially when you want to quit, is invaluable. The friend you choose should be someone who will ask you how it's going, what you're learning, and help you process what God taught you during the fast. If you want them to encourage you and spur you on and all they do is say, "You still fasting?... good," then I'd suggest finding someone who can ask better questions such as: How is the fast going? What is God teaching you? What have you experienced during the fast that has been surprising? Difficult? Awesome? Have you received any clarity on your focus? If so, how? If no, what are you still processing?

Of course, these questions are things you should process on your own, but the opportunity to talk to someone can help you see what you may have missed and will assist you in thinking deeper about what God is doing. Whether you find someone to fast with you, or just support you through your fast, make sure to let them know your focus so they can pray specifically for your focus. You can ask them to call or text you randomly while they are praying as a way to cheer you on and remind you they are speaking to God on your behalf. Having someone fast with you brings a higher level of accountability since they have decided to sacrifice for you. It can also provide greater clarity on your focus. You will have multiple sets of ears listening for God's guidance for you.

Prayer

Lastly, as you decide how and when to fast, do so in prayer. Your motivation going into, and throughout your fast can make your experience great or a complete waste of time. If you think fasting is kind of neat, and a great way to lose some weight, or is just giving something up for the sake of mental strength, then the results of your fast will fall far short of what it could be. Entering into a fast with a focus on God and a desire to clear away distractions for the sake of making God your greatest need will allow you to get the most out of your experience.

Prepare your heart, mind, and body with prayer. When hunger pangs hit or the desire to watch sports becomes strong, use those as cues to sink into God's Word and into prayer. This will mean you'll probably be praying a lot and spending a lot more time with God. If your motivation is right, these are good things. If your motivation is wrong, these senses will be frustrating urges. Preparing your heart in prayer before and during the fast will help refocus your motivation on the right thing.

Unfortunately, many people think fasting is for the spiritually elite and miss out on a fantastic opportunity to develop their relationship with God through this challenging but extremely valuable discipline. Don't skip out on this discipline because it's hard. Jesus expected His followers to fast because He knew that fasting can create a more intimate connection with Him.

Questions For Reflection:

- Have you ever fasted?

- Write down what you remember about your fast or, if you haven't fasted, write about the fears you have about fasting.

> *Entering into a fast with a focus on God and a desire to clear away distractions for the sake of making God your greatest need will allow you to get the most out of your experience.*

- If you were to fast, what would you fast from and what would you fast for?

- Have you ever known anyone who has fasted? Ask them about their experience.

Chapter 14

Solitude

How would you respond if I told you to go somewhere free of distractions, free of your phone, and spend some time alone to focus on God? Maybe you hear that, and your eyes get big, and your heart starts beating a little faster because you know that would be glorious! Maybe your eyes get big and your heart starts beating a little quicker because you think that would be horrible! For some, the discipline of solitude is celebrated and eagerly anticipated. For others, the idea of being alone makes your palms sweat, and you've already thought, "what's the shortest necessary time for solitude."

What Is Solitude?

Solitude is the discipline of removing yourself from others to spend time with God. The intent of solitude is not so much about being alone, although that is part of the process. The focus is being with and connecting to God, one-on-one. We live in a time where noise and distractions are everywhere, even when we don't want them. Most mornings, before my kids wake, before the chaos of the day starts, I get up to read my Bible and pray.

Despite these less-distracting circumstances, my phone still silently beckons me to scroll. One of my kids will wake up early. I'll be eager to start work, or my loving wife will need to update me on

> *Solitude is the discipline of removing yourself from others to spend time with God.*

her dream from the night before. These are just a few of the things that can encroach on my time with God and distract me from connecting with Him. My guess is your experience is not much different. Solitude deals with the distractions by inviting you to leave your chaos, your work, and your busyness, to settle in the presence of God. Solitude means going to, or creating, a setting free from interruptions so you can spend undistracted time with the most interesting, powerful, all-knowing, wise, and loving God.

No matter how you feel about extracting yourself from distractions to hear from God—excited, anxious, or in between—solitude is a discipline that every Christian should practice. The only evidence needed to show that solitude is a discipline of pinnacle importance is the fact that Jesus practiced solitude. Jesus took time away to connect with God the Father. And He and the Father are ONE!

Jesus' ministry began by spending 40 days in solitude (and fasting). Throughout His life, Jesus removed Himself from the crowds to clear the clutter and connect with God. Every one of the gospel writers includes statements of Jesus withdrawing for a time of solitude.

"As soon as Jesus heard the news, he left in a boat to a remote area to be alone." (Mt. 14:13).

"But Jesus often withdrew to the wilderness for prayer." (Lk. 5:16).

"Before daybreak the next morning, Jesus got up and went out to an isolated place to pray." (Mk. 1:35).

If Jesus, God Himself, needed times of solitude, and He is connected to the Father more intimately than anyone in history, then the need for you to spend time in solitude, to bond with Him, is even more vital.

> *Jesus took time away to connect with God the Father. And He and the Father are ONE!*

How To Solitude

The key to solitude is getting away from distractions and finding ways to center your thoughts on God. Whether it's a park, the beach, mountains, or lake, getting out in nature is probably your best bet for a good time of solitude. Placing yourself in God's creation can help draw you to His grandeur and beauty. It also eliminates the interruptions of advertisements, angry drivers, or misbehaving kids.

Wherever you go, make sure to put your cell phone on "Do not disturb" (or turn it off), because no matter how far you are from other distractions, your phone is always screaming, "LISTEN TO ME. FORGET WHAT YOU'RE DOING. I'M MORE IMPORTANT."

Eliminating distractions is not just about what you get away from. It's about what you're moving toward: a conversation with God. Sitting out in nature for an extended time may help you focus on God. On the other hand, it could be terribly distracting because sitting still stirs a million random thoughts, making it super challenging to focus on God. Maybe solitude is most valuable when you are actively involved in hiking, bike riding, or doing some artwork.

Being alone to be with God can take many different forms. I encourage you to find a way to have solitude that eliminates distractions and helps you have meaningful conversations with God. If that means reading your Bible for hours, great! If you need to listen to an audio Bible, sermon, or worship music, great! If it means lying on the beach and having an internal dialogue and prayer time with God, great!

> *Eliminating distractions is not just about what you get away from. It's about what you're moving toward: a conversation with God.*

Whichever way you practice solitude, find a way to ruthlessly eliminate the things that pull you away from focusing on God. Don't rush, and don't get frustrated. Know that even if your times with God seem inefficient, there is nothing inefficient about a heart that wants to spend time with Him. Even if you don't have a life-changing interaction, just the act of giving God your time will effect you!

Length Of Solitude

There are no hard and fast rules for the length of time you need to spend in solitude. It may be a week, a weekend, a day, an hour, or something in-between. If you have a week to spend in solitude, that's awesome, but my guess is you need to start much smaller. Solitude is less about the amount of time and more about the quality of the time. Remember, it's about eliminating distractions to elevate communication with God. Whatever time you have to give to solitude, start there, but don't stop there. If an hour is easy for you, see if you can make it to an hour and a half. If that's easy, see if you can make it a few hours. Stretching yourself beyond comfort may give more space for your communication with God to develop.

In my experience, the discomfort of extending my solitude with God has been both frustrating and growth-inducing. I would rather spend five minutes reading my Bible, writing quickly in my journal, getting a nugget of inspiration from God, and moving on. Sitting for a more prolonged amount of time forces me to soak in what I'm doing, not allowing me to speed through, and drawing me to more profound reflection. I have to sit with my thoughts, thoughts that I've prayed would be filled with God's voice, to contemplate what He is saying. More extensive periods of solitude have also filled my soul with tension because I begin to long for the distractions I've removed myself from. If you find yourself feeling the same way, allow these tensions to be a launching point for a more in-depth discussion with God. "Why is this so frustrating and difficult?" "Why do I crave my distractions more than God?" "Why is spending time with God less satisfying than ____?" Rushing through a time of solitude may be fruitful but stretching your time will foster a more transformative interaction with God.

Like fasting, your time of solitude should always have a focus. Getting away just to "get away" can be refreshing, but Biblical solitude has a primary, and sometimes a secondary, focus. The primary intention of solitude is to spend time and connect with God. Solitude is a date with God. I spend plenty of time with my wife, and we talk every single day. Yet, we regularly schedule extra time and spend extra money to break from the patterns and distractions of life to talk more intimately and enjoy the exclusiveness of just the two of us. Ask any marriage counselor, and they will tell you regular date nights are crucial to the growth and health of a relationship. This is no different from our relationship with God. Do I talk with God regularly? Yes. Is God with me all the time? Yes. But there is massive value in setting aside time for Him and me to talk in a different, distraction-less environment.

The secondary focus can be any number of things, from asking God to give you direction for a decision or desiring to more fully understand one of His attributes. Solitude dispels the disruptions so you can more clearly hear His response and know Him more.

Reminder: As with many of these disciplines, you have to schedule time with God, just like my date nights with my wife have to be scheduled. If you think that you'll "find the time," you are fooling yourself. Even though date nights and solitude are essential, life tends to squeeze them out with busyness, projects, and "something came up." Be diligent in setting aside regular times of solitude with God, and keep your time sacred, no matter what.

Questions For Reflection:

- When was the last time you had a time of solitude (whether to focus on God or not)?

- Does time alone excite you or drive you nuts? Why?

- The purpose of Christian solitude isn't to be alone; it's to be alone with God. What would it look like to have fruitful solitude with God? What would you need/need to do?

- What is keeping you from regular solitude with God, and how can you eliminate that barrier?

Chapter 15

Celebration

Strangers hugged each other, people jumped up and down, and the noise was so loud I couldn't even hear the sound of my own cheers. I've never been to an event that was so overwhelmed by celebration. The place was HP Pavilion, and the event was game seven of the 2008 conference quarterfinals of the NHL playoffs. The San Jose Sharks beat the Calgary Flames 5-3. I love ice hockey, and each goal the Sharks scored set the "Shark Tank" into a frenzy. I'm guessing you are somewhat familiar with ice hockey, but let me give you a quick overview of what it is. Ice hockey is two teams dressed up in different colors, gliding around on ice, sometimes getting in fist-fights, and using sticks to hit a puck into a goal. Sounds odd, huh? There is a bit more to it, but it really boils down to that description. And yet, there I was, with 20,000 other people, going berserk about the little black disk going into the other team's net.

I hope you can recall a time in your life where you were so filled with elation and excitement that your natural reaction was celebration. No one had to tell you, "you should really celebrate what just happened." But the spiritual discipline of celebration is needed because the elation of a moment can quickly pass (as I realized with the Sharks losing in the next round). You need to be grounded in the truth of God's goodness and love all the time, not just when you feel like it.

Party Time!

To understand the disciple of celebration, you first must know that the intention of celebration isn't to conjure excitement but to remind you of God's goodness and provision. Throughout the Old Testament, regular celebrations were established to call people back to these truths. The holiday of Purim celebrates the Jewish deliverance from Haman (see Est. 9:27). The Passover meal celebrates God sparing Israel's children from death and delivering Israel from slavery (see Ex. 12). The Feast of Weeks celebrates the first fruits of the harvest (see Ex. 34). These are just a few, and each one was founded for Israel to pause, remember, and celebrate God's goodness. These celebrations refocused Israel on the truth of what God had done to strengthen their faith in what God promised to do. Celebrations reminded Israel of who God is: good, loving, and sovereign.

As you read the Old Testament, you may scoff at the Israelite's amnesia regarding God's faithfulness. Even with so many celebratory reminders of what God had done, they continually and quickly forgot. Before you get too worked up about their issues, I think if we're honest, our actions and attitudes too often reflect Israel's forgetfulness. When life is good, we do our own thing, allowing God to hang around just in case anything goes wrong, but we don't rely on Him daily. Then, life gets tough. We forget all of God's previous and current blessings, quickly growing frustrated with Him for not solving our problems.

Celebration fights both of these traps, moving you to a stronger foundation in Him. When you practice celebration in the good times, it calls you back to remembering that each blessing is undeservedly given to you by God. Celebration reminds you not to take those blessings for granted. When you practice celebration in the tough times, it reminds you that God is good and worthy of your praise despite life's trials. Celebration helps you discover the things you can praise God for in the hardships. Celebration reminds you of the good things God has blessed you with in the past and the promises He has for your future. When you celebrate, no matter what season you are in, you grow in your faith in God and your conviction of His goodness.

How To Celebrate

Just do it. Celebration comes naturally in times of great excitement, so take note of how you've celebrated things in the past and then use your natural celebration as a pattern for your relationship with God. Seriously. I'm sure you celebrate a few birthdays each

> *Celebration helps you discover the things you can praise God for in the hardships, reminds you of the good things God has blessed you with in the past, and looks towards the promises He has for your future.*

year with food, friends, gifts. So why not once a year throw a God party. I know that sounds cheesy, but it doesn't have to be.

Make good food, have a delicious dessert, and have people share stories of how they have seen God work in their lives and others' lives in the past year. My family and I have a "Thankful box," where, through the year, we place little reminder cards of our favorite memories. At the end of the year, we take about a week to read through them, celebrating all God's blessings.

Celebration doesn't just have to be an event you create; it can be part of something you're already doing. My excitement over the Sharks winning translates to the fact that sometimes during worship, I find myself jumping up and down or clapping in celebration of the God to whom I'm singing to. Maybe during a hike, you pause to stand in awe of the beauty around you, and you speak out loud your thankfulness and praise to God for His creation. Often while I'm playing hockey, I celebrate, in my mind, the ability to exercise in such a fun way. You can also journal your celebration and invite others to celebrate with you by sharing what you've written. There is no exact way to celebrate, but true celebration needs to be focused on remembering God's goodness and praising Him.

The discipline of celebration in tough times can include the previous expressions but is often less exuberant and more of posturing your heart to remember and proclaim God's goodness. It's not a "fake it till you make it" action of pretending to be excited about life when it stinks. In difficult times, celebration means being honest about how you're feeling while calling yourself back to the truth that God is good and loving. Even when you don't feel like you have anything to celebrate, focus your celebration on the fact that the pains of this earth will someday be removed for an eternity of unbelievable joy. Celebrate that Jesus didn't stay dead, and because He rose from the dead, you have hope in the midst of whatever you're going through.

Celebration can be so much fun, reminding you of the great joy you have in Jesus. It can also be challenging in tough times, a struggle to give God praise. Wherever you find yourself, don't miss the opportunities to celebrate God in both big and small ways.

Celebrate what He's done. Celebrate what He is doing. Celebrate what He will do. God invites you to enjoy Him and to enjoy life. I pray your life is marked by an abundance of celebration. After all, the fact that God came to this earth, died for your sins and rose from the dead is worth WAY more celebration than a hockey puck slipping past an opponent's goalie. We'll be celebrating God for eternity... Why not start now?

Questions For Reflection:

- What questions do you have about this discipline?

- How can you incorporate this discipline into your life?

- A Christian's life should be filled with celebration. Why do you think we're not known for our celebration, and how can you be a person known for living in celebration?

- How would your relationship with God be affected if you practiced celebration more?

Chapter 16

Serving

"Hey J.P., can you help me out with this electrical issue?"

"Sure."

"Hey J.P., would you be willing to mentor some college students?"

"I'd be honored."

"Hey J.P., we need someone to organize a service project."

"I got it."

"Hey J.P., can you serve _____"

"Yes"

J.P. is a close friend of mine and someone who embodies the heart of a servant. Often, when I have an opportunity to serve, I think of how he would respond, and the answer is clearly, "yes." The thing with J.P. is his service is not just completing a task. He serves with love and compassion, and he would tell you he is merely distributing the love and grace he has received from God. Service is not a responsibility; it is his natural response to what God has done in his life. As we discuss the discipline of service, your motivation has to be the same: as a response, not a responsibility. Let's look at how this plays out as you serve.

More Like Christ= More Like A Servant

Being a servant and regularly serving is an integral part of following Christ. You can't become more like Christ and not serve. Jesus was the embodiment of sacrificial, loving service. Philippians 2:1-7 explains:

> *You can't become more like Christ and not serve.*

"So if there is any encouragement in Christ, any comfort from love, any participation in the Spirit, any affection and sympathy, complete my joy by being of the same mind, having the same love, being in full accord and of one mind. Do nothing from selfish ambition or conceit, but in humility count others more significant than yourselves. Let each of you look not only to his own interests, but also to the interests of others. Have this mind among yourselves, which is yours in Christ Jesus, who, though he was in the form of God, did not count equality with God a thing to be grasped, but emptied himself, by taking the form of a servant, being born in the likeness of men." (ESV)

Jesus' entire life was dedicated to serving others. As God, He had the right to come to earth with worldly authority, living in comfortable luxury and power, forcing everyone to serve Him. Instead, He came as a helpless baby, born to a poor, ostracized couple, and grew up to be a homeless wanderer. Jesus lived His life to reveal the fullness of God's love to everyone. He expressed ultimate servitude by being beaten, mocked, abused, and killed for our sins.

Loving and serving others is not a "take it or leave it" suggestion. It is a discipline Jesus fully lived out and commanded His followers to practice. Jesus clearly explains His expectation of service to His disciples in the book of Mark.

"So Jesus called them together and said, "You know that the rulers in this world lord it over their people, and officials flaunt their authority over those under them. But among you it will be different. Whoever wants to be a leader among you must be your servant, and whoever wants to be first among you must be the slave of everyone else. For even the Son of Man came not to be served but to serve others and to give his life as a ransom for many" (10:42-45).

By serving others, you show them Christ-like love and expose them to the truth of God's redemptive plan. Serving others also affirms the value they have in Christ by giving them a taste of what God did for them on the

> *Loving and serving others is not a "take it or leave it" suggestion. It is a discipline Jesus fully lived out and commanded His followers to practice.*

cross. If there were no other reasons to serve, these reasons would be enough, but in God's loving economy, there are benefits He provides for you when you serve. Mainly, as you serve, you grow. Godly service fights your human selfishness and makes you more Christ-like. To be more like Christ is the greatest blessing you can receive, but God's blessings don't stop there.

Serving invites you to experience God in more profound ways as you will need to rely on Him to continue to lay down your life for others. Your spiritual maturity will develop because serving is putting into action what you believe. By serving, God's love becomes a living, present, tangible action in your life. When you serve, you are both participating in and experiencing God working through you.

Not A Burden, An Opportunity

Unfortunately, "opportunities to serve" is often heard as burdensome, guilt-inducing responsibility. Instead, the opportunities to serve should be heard and engaged in with excitement and conviction. Knowing what God has done for you, and His promise to be with you, should stir an eagerness to serve. Believing that Jesus gave up everything, to the point of unbelievable pain, should give you a healthy conviction to serve, no matter the cost. This does not mean serving won't be hard (remember what Christ went through to serve you=excruciating).

It does mean you should count it a blessing to walk in humble obedience as Christ did—by helping others—even when it's tough. Serving means you get to spend your life on the most important thing ever—building God's Kingdom—and in the process, you get to learn and grow in your relationship with God. When seen in the correct perspective, it baffles my mind that churches worldwide have to work so hard to convince people to serve (both inside and outside the church.) Serving is one of the primary reactions to following Christ.

Serving Symptom

Like a kid who says he needs to stay home from school but doesn't display any signs of sickness, many people claim they follow Jesus but show no signs of His heart. Is there a reason to be skeptical? Having Jesus in your life should produce some sort of serving symptom. I don't mean this to be a guilt-ridden reprimand, but an eye-opening reality check. Maybe you've wished you were growing in your relationship with God, sensing His presence more, and seeing more evidence of Him in your life. Perhaps this is an opportunity to evaluate your life and ask if you're serving others in such a way where all those things are a desperate need and not a wishful want. Maybe you've become comfortable continuing to hear about God's love while not allowing it to move you to act out His love, by serving others. Perhaps the very desire for closeness and growth with God is being hindered by an unwillingness to live the life to which He has called you.

Hyperventilation And Reasons Not To Serve

I've had two panic attacks in my life, and both were during the swimming portion of a triathlon. Surrounded by hundreds of swimmers jostling for position, kicking me in the face, my competitiveness drove me to swim harder than I had practiced. The chaos of so many people, the reality that I was in the middle of the ocean, and the fear of death all set my swim stroke out of rhythm, and my breathing became erratic. Each time my head came out of the water, I gasped for more air as my mind screamed, "You can't breathe!" No matter what I did, I couldn't get enough air. I literally thought to myself, "Do I call the lifeguard over, or will they see me floating face down and come rescue me?" I was overwhelmed with terror, and had to stop swimming, still trying to gulp down air, and settle my frenzied mind from the panic. At the height of my terror I remembered some advice I'd received about hyperventilation, "You feel like you need more air, but you actually need to get rid of air." I put my head down in the water, so I couldn't breathe in and forced a lungful of air out. My mind said, "This is stupid, you need air," but I had to trust the advice I was given. After a few rounds of focusing on breathing out, not in, my breathing settled, my mind stopped panicking, and I could continue the swim and finish the race. After the race, I reflected on how odd it was that my body told me to do the exact opposite of what I needed to do (keep sucking in more air) to continue and thrive. This is the same for serving.

Many people's spiritual lives are stifled or dying because they live with an assumption that they need more teaching, more worship, and more consumption of Christianity before serving. A "breathing in" of all these things is good—very good—but if there is no output, no "breathing out," you become trapped in an unhealthy, life-sucking, dangerous pattern that suffocates your spiritual life.

I don't remember where I heard the advice about hyperventilation, but having that warning saved me from something much worse. Similarly, the awareness I'm about to bring to some barriers to serving is given with the hope that it keeps you from spiraling into the dangers of complacency and inaction.

"I don't know all the Bible," "I'm not smart enough," "I don't have time," are the three reasons I most often hear for not serving; for continuing the unhealthy process of breathing in without breathing out.

"I Don't Know All The Bible"

The danger of "I don't know all the Bible" is that it's true. Of course, you don't know all of the Bible. Of course, you'll come across things which confuse you. Of course, there will be questions you can't answer. There might be things children learned when they were in kindergarten that a 35-year-old might hear for the first time. That's okay. You may come across stories that surprise you which a middle schooler can easily explain. That's fine. Even if you were to memorize the entire Bible, there would still be things to learn and discover. Everyone lacks a fully comprehensive understanding of the Bible.

When I was in seminary, I had some brilliant professors who knew how to read and speak the original languages of the Bible. They knew the historical context of each book. Their knowledge amazed me. Even though they are more knowledgeable about the

Bible than I ever could be, they are still learning and growing. Even they experience new discoveries of things they never saw before. God doesn't say, "You need to reach a 'pastor-level understanding' of the Bible to serve." God will use you, as you are—with the gifts, talents, and knowledge you have—to build His Kingdom. Don't let, "I don't know all the Bible," to keep you from serving.

"I'm Not Smart Enough"

"I'm not smart enough." Again, this is true. You aren't. I'm not. My professors aren't. Not being "smart enough" isn't a reason not to serve. Here is something you must understand as you serve: you are called to serve, but any actual spiritual growth happens because God works through you. In the same chapter as the verse you read at the beginning of this section, Paul said, "Dear friends, you always followed my instructions when I was with you. And now that I am away, it is even more important. Work hard to show the results of your salvation, obeying God with deep reverence and fear. For God is working in you, giving you the desire and the power to do what pleases him" (Phil. 2:12-13).

In other words, you don't need to rely on yourself and your "smartness" to be qualified to serve. You need to depend on God because He is the one working in and through you. These truths should bring a great sense of relief and thrill. Relief that you don't have to have a Ph.D. and a thrill that you get to partner with God to serve others. Should you keep striving to gain Biblical knowledge? Absolutely, but don't allow "I'm not smart enough" to stop you from doing what God has called you to and missing out on the opportunity for God to grow you.

> *You don't need to rely on yourself and your "smartness" to be qualified to serve. You need to depend on God.*

"I Don't Have Time"

I've addressed this type of statement earlier in the critique on busyness. Still, it's such an epidemic that I want to briefly remind you of what I said. A statement about your time is a statement about your values. If someone were to offer you loads of money to free your calendar each week for a certain amount of time, you'd probably easily find space to do so. This is because the value of loads of money is worth it. So, when you use the excuse, "I don't have time," you're really saying, "I don't value what God has asked of me. I don't value the eternal benefits of being obedient to God in the opportunity to serve others."

Remember, Jesus doesn't suggest you serve. He doesn't say, "As long as you're not busy, then it'd be great for you to serve a little." He says, "if you love me, you will keep my commands" (Jn. 14:15), and one of His commands is, "Love others as I have loved you." (Jn. 13:34)

Jesus was a model of sacrificial, serving love. Therefore, you are to serve others. If "busyness" has kept you from serving, I want to encourage you to fight against that excuse by remembering the eternal value of serving. Nothing you do is more important than loving God, and loving God means loving others. You cannot separate the two. As you practice the discipline of serving, you have to be careful to not make serving about "just doing your time." Serving is not about putting in the hours so you can be "good with God," or so you don't feel guilty.

The spiritual discipline of service is not just signing up and showing up. It's about having the heart to show others God's pursuing, sacrificial love. If you

> *The spiritual discipline of service is not just signing up and showing up. It's about having the heart to show others God's pursuing, sacrificial love.*

serve only to fill a role, God can use you, and He may grow you, but you will miss out on the much greater opportunity for growth. Serving with a heart to show God's love, with a willing response to what He has done for you, is the heart of service God desires. This doesn't mean that serving comes easy. If it came easy, Jesus wouldn't have had to talk about it so much.

Whatever reason you've given to not regularly serve, silence your excuses by reflecting on how Jesus has served you and calls you to serve others. Then live out the challenge James makes in his letter:

"What good is it, dear brothers and sisters, if you say you have faith but don't show it by your actions? Can that kind of faith save anyone? Suppose you see a brother or sister who has no food or clothing, and you say, "Good-bye and have a good day; stay warm and eat well"—but then you don't give that person any food or clothing. What good does that do? So you see, faith by itself isn't enough. Unless it produces good deeds, it is dead and useless" (Jas. 2:14-17).

How To Serve

Look for opportunities and respond. There are plenty of ways to serve, both in and out of the church. Don't expect opportunities to just fall into your lap. Figure out your talents and resources and seek (or create) chances to use them. Don't be so rigid in your ideal way of serving that you aren't open to allowing God to use you in unexpected ways. Not all service is doing something you were "made for." You shouldn't wait for the serving opportunity that fulfills you in every way. I don't think that any area of serving is the "perfect fit." Serving is hard work, and every area of service will have difficulties, but it would be a terrible loss for you, and for the body of believers, if you allow any hardship to keep you from doing what God has called you to.

An easy place to start serving is finding a ministry in the church, but you don't have to wait for the church to start serving. Build a relationship with someone younger in the faith and serve them by mentoring them. Connect with a neighbor and help them with yard work or house projects. Invite a neighbor over regularly for a meal or mow their lawn. Bring a gift to a friend in need. Be the room parent for your child's classroom and find ways to serve the other parents and kids in your child's class. Serve at a local home-less shelter once a month. You could _____.

Whatever you do, do it with a desire for those you are serving to come to know and love Jesus. When you serve, go above and beyond. Instead of serving once a month at church or in the shelter, serve once a week. Seek to have deep intentional conversations with those you serve. Instead of just mentoring a younger Christian, buy them coffee or dinner, invite them to be part of your family vaca-tions. For your neighbor, respond to a need without them asking, and ask your friends how you can serve them and pray for them, regularly.

Jesus left the glory of heaven to become a dirty, needy man who was mocked, beaten, spit on, and crucified all for the sake of glorifying the Father. Jesus served you, and His most significant act of service cost him his life. May you look to His act for the strength to serve those around you. May you reflect His sacrificial, serving love in a way that invites the world to know how great He is, and grows you to look more and more like Him.*

*Find out more about how God has gifted you in the Spiritual Gifts section

Questions For Reflection:

- If you are serving somewhere, what is the best part about serving, and what is the most challenging part?

- How have you grown through serving?

- If you aren't serving somewhere, what is keeping you from it?

- What talents and resources do you have that you can use to serve others?

- Would others look at how you spend your time and resources and say, "you are a servant"? Why or why not?

Chapter 17

Guidance

Imagine needing to make a big decision in life. Maybe it's a career change, a cross-country move, a commitment to marriage, or even whether or not to have a challenging discussion with a friend. Each of these decisions (and many others) weighs heavy on the soul and can be very difficult to navigate. If you've faced any of these, my guess is you've sought guidance from others. Big decisions are tough, but they can be excruciating if you have no one with whom you can dialogue and seek advice. On the other hand, receiving counsel and discussing choices with even one other person can bring considerable clarity and calm to life's tensions. Guidance is the invitation to have others participate in your decisions, both big and small.

While God does speak to you directly, through His Word and the Holy Spirit's convictions, the discipline of guidance allows others to be God's mouthpiece to help you hear and discern His voice.

Guidance seeks godly wisdom, correction, and direction from others. One crucial element in growing in your understanding, obedience, and love of God is receiving guidance from fellow Christians. On one level, you receive guidance every time you hear God's Word preached. Sunday messages or podcasts are helpful tools, but those one-way communication venues can only go so far in guiding you. When was the last time you faced a tough decision or thought you heard God prompt you to do something and raised your hand in the middle of the church service to ask the pastor what he thinks you should do? Probably never, but the answers to those questions are super important, maybe even more important than the topic the pastor is speaking about that week.

> *Guidance seeks godly wisdom, correction, and direction from others.*

God's Voice Through Others

God wants a personal relationship with you, which means...He wants to interact with you personally. One way God interacts with you more personally is through His church—the body of believers. Paul clarifies the purpose of the church isn't to have a pastor preach well (although that is a good thing) but "to equip God's people to do his work and build up the church, the body of Christ. This will continue until we all come to such unity in our faith and knowledge of God's Son that we will be mature in the Lord, measuring up to the full and complete standard of Christ." (Eph. 4:12-13). God wants you, wants us, to build one another up, guiding each other to the fullness of faith and knowledge of the Gospel.

Guidance is not just a discipline to receive; it is a discipline to offer. As you accept Christ into your life and commit to following Him, you are called to make disciples. As believers in Christ, each one of us is commanded (not just church staff; each of us) to participate in the lives of others to help them listen, respond to, and live out the Gospel. To do this properly, we must seek God, input His Word into our lives, and rely on Him as we offer guidance to others.

I've been a pastor for over 14 years and a Christian for over 30. During my life and throughout my career, I've read the Bible, spent significant time in prayer, fasted, and listened to countless sermons. Each of these elements has helped me grow in my relationship with Jesus, but my most significant growth has happened because an older, wiser mentor took time to guide me. I would not be where I am today without men like Adam Miller, Steve Clifford, and Nathan Smith. These men have listened to me, prayed for me, rooted themselves in God's Word, and offered God-ordained guidance throughout my life. Guidance has been central to my faith development, and I pray that you will do whatever it takes to place people in your life that can help guide you in your journey.

> *As believers in Christ, each one of us is commanded to participate in the lives of others to help them listen, respond to, and live out the Gospel.*

How To Practice Guidance

The promotion of individualism has seeped into the Christian culture. A "personal relationship with God" has been misunderstood to mean that all that matters is your individual interaction with Him. From the very beginning, this is not how God created us to function in His Kingdom. While the following verses are focused on man/woman relationship, one of the principles it exposes us to can be applied to all relationships. The Bible tells us that "God formed the man from the dust of the ground," (Gen. 2:7) and soon after, God says, "it is not good for the man to be alone" (Gen. 2:18).

This may seem like an insignificant detail, but God's statement in Genesis 2:18 is huge when you realize that when God said these words, man had Him (God) as a companion. You would think if man had God as a companion, God would say, "man is not alone." God created us for a second connection—each other. God crafted us to enjoy one another, refine one another, and encourage one another. Unfortunately, because of sin, the unadulterated interaction with one another was broken, and the first response to sin is a movement toward individualism "She did it...It wasn't me...I had no part of it" (Gen. 3:12). I share this because, to practice guidance, you have to fight for it. At our core, we long for deeper connections. We long for people in our life to encourage and refine us. This is how we were made. Yet, there is something at war with these ideals: pride, selfishness, laziness, anger, apathy. Sin caused the tension between what we were made for and how we live. If we don't fight against this, sin will move us away from the crucial discipline of guidance.

As important as guidance is, please don't think that the church is responsible for providing you with the right person/people to guide you. While a church may give some suggestions or may offer opportunities to connect, developing a relationship to receive guidance requires YOU seeking out and asking others for this. Meeting with your pastor may not be something you can do as often as you need, so don't forget this truth: The body of believers, not just the pastors, is there to build one another up, to guide each other to Christ-likeness.

Since guidance goes beyond pastoral counseling, the best way to seek it, is to ask. Ask an older, wiser Christian. Ask the people you meet on Sunday. Ask the greeters. Ask someone in your community group. Ask them, "Can we meet so I can get some guidance in my life?" or ask them, "Who can I meet with to get some guidance in my life?"*

*As a warning, it may take a few different tries and some time to find the right person, but don't give up. If the process stalls, simply start building relationships with people, and when you find someone who is wise, ask that person to be a guide to you.

When you meet for guidance, spend time in prayer and ask the person guiding you to spend time in prayer as you talk about life, tensions, decisions, and direction. Then talk about those things. Talk about what you've been processing. Share your heart, where you think God might be directing things, where He has been challenging you, and your raw emotions—good or bad. Allow the person guiding you to hear your heart and not a façade of holiness.

Remember, God already knows your heart and putting on false holiness to impress the person who is guiding you will stifle growth. Ask questions of the person guiding you, and then listen as they respond. If you trust their connection to God and have asked that they prayerfully listen, then what they say may be God's personal response to you.**

**If you are given advice that contradicts scripture, stop seeking guidance from that person, and let him know where you see inconsistencies between their direction and the Bible. Your honesty will give them a chance to learn, clarify misunderstandings, or expose a discrepancy that needs to be dealt with. If they were recommended by a church program/leadership, then inform the overseeing leader as well.

As I said before, guidance is not just something to receive, it is also something to offer. This is what this book is all about. It gives you the tools to fully live out your faith, AND it equips you to guide, mentor, encourage, and disciple others. The book's final section will focus on some practical ways to disciple others, but the rule of "Ask" still applies. Don't wait for a program or for the church to ask you to engage in serving and guiding others. Instead, be the torchbearer for guiding others. Ask, ask, ask. Ask the church, "Is there anyone that I can pour into?"*** Ask those you know who are younger or newer in the faith, "Would you like to meet regularly to talk about life and faith?" Ask friends and family if they know anyone you could encourage and mentor...then, relying on God, do it.

> *Don't wait for a program or for the church to ask you to engage in serving and guiding others.*

***The church should have a vetting process to make sure that you share their beliefs and can guide others. Don't take this as an insult. It is a process to help protect people, and if the church says you're not ready, then trust the leadership and seek more guidance for yourself.

Questions For Reflection:

- Have you ever sought guidance from another Christian? What was that like?

- Have you ever offered guidance to someone else? What was that like?

- Is there someone in your life right now from whom you can seek guidance? What do you need to do to make that happen?

- Is there someone in your life right now to whom you can offer guidance? What do you need to do to make that happen?

- What are some qualities that describe the perfect mentor/ guide? Seek that out.

PART THREE

Drive the Truck
(Applying What You've Learned)

I had been given the keys to my Dad's truck and was expected to be home before curfew. Months of driver's education, behind the wheel instruction, driving with a permit and tests, gave me the tools I needed to take this beautiful 1982 Datsun King Cab out on the road alone. Without hesitation, I buckled up and joyfully put to use all I had learned, and the experience was amazing. Yes, scary at times, and I definitely had more to learn, but that didn't stop me from the thrilling experience of driving on my own.

Now imagine, with all the training, tests, and time behind the wheel, I refused the opportunity to take out my Dad's truck, settling for more training and tests. At first, you may say I was wise (although, by all measurements, I proved proficiency), but if this hesitancy carried on for a month or more, you would rightly question what I'm doing. I know my parents would be frustrated with my unwillingness to use my ability (as well having to continue to drive me everywhere).

In the same way, the remaining chapters of this book are all about taking the package of what you've learned so far, everything you've learned about Jesus throughout your life, and putting it into action to make disciples. Jesus' parting words to His disciples were the launching pad for the ministry we are called to continue: "I have been given all authority in heaven and on earth. Therefore, go and make disciples of all the nations, baptizing them in the name of the Father and the Son and the Holy Spirit. Teach these new disciples to obey all the commands I have given you. And be sure of this: I am with you always, even to the end of the age." (Mt. 28:18-20). In other words, "Drive the truck!"

Chapter 18

Spiritual Gifts

"Mom, I don't want to go to hell."

Sometime around the age of five, I became aware of the reality of eternity, and in particular, hell...and I knew I did not want to go there.

"Drew, you don't have to. Jesus died for you, and if you put your trust in Him, you will have eternal life."

"I really want that. Can I pray with you now?"

My fear led me to pray with my Mom, asking Jesus into my heart...and begging Him to keep me out of that bad place. After a few nights of the same pleading prayer, my Mom reassured me that the first prayer did the job, settling my insecurities. Still, for many years my motivation for following Jesus revolved around where I would go when I died. While heaven will be eternally marvelous, the focus of my life after death had me missing out on opportunities to experience God's presence in my life...before death.

The Promise For Now, Not Just Death

When you decide to follow Jesus, you aren't only assured of something when you die, you are given an incredible gift to be used now. God sends His Spirit to you to help guide you and empower you to do the supernatural work of building His Kingdom. Every single follower of Christ has access to the Holy Spirit to make an eternal impact on humanity. Jesus is so confident in the work of the Holy Spirit that He tells His followers, "'I tell you the truth, anyone who believes in me will do the same works I have done, *and even greater works*, because I am going to be with the Father." (Jn. 14:12).

The implications of this statement are immense. Jesus had a history-changing ministry. He healed the sick, raised the dead, convinced people to give up all their worldly pursuits to follow Him, loved in a way the world had never seen, and so much more. He was able to do great things, and yet, this verse records Him telling His followers that they will be able to do "greater works." God wants to give you the joy of His presence in heaven, but He also gives you the joy of His presence now...to do greater works.

Greater Works

Essentially Jesus is saying, if you've entrusted your life to Him, then the impact of your relationship with Him, with His Spirit in you, has the potential for "even greater works than these." Pause a second and let that truth sink in. It's important to know that the power to do greater works is not due to your own strength, knowledge, or perseverance. The ability comes from the Holy Spirit. God's

Spirit is in you! That is an outstanding, life-altering truth! When you understand Jesus' statement within the larger Biblical context, the "WOW" of His promise becomes even more impressive. Let me explain.

During all of Israel's history, only a tiny group of people could enter into the Holy of Holies—the space where God's Spirit manifested. The select few who could enter did so with fear,

> *The power to do greater works is not due to your own strength, knowledge, or perseverance. The ability comes from the Holy Spirit.*

knowing they would die if they did not properly prepare themselves to interact with God. The High Priest was a unique, set apart, holy person who had both the privilege and the weight of presenting prayers and special sacrifices to God. These priests were the only ones with direct access to God. The temple/priest system was the primary way God interacted with His people before Jesus. Now, Jesus tells His followers that there will be a change. Instead of a select few, all those who love Him will be given God's Spirit to personally interact with. Jesus is flipping the script. Interaction with God isn't for the special few who are holy enough to enter into a place where God resides. Instead, God will make His residence (by His Holy Spirit) in every person who believes in Jesus.

Maybe the significance of this is better understood with this analogy. When I was younger, I loved the 49ers, particularly Jerry Rice (the best wide receiver in the history of football). I was always a wide receiver when we played football at the park. I got his jersey for Christmas, which I rarely wore due to an unreasonable fear of ruining it. I practiced diving catches to look like him. I often imagined myself as him—catching the winning touchdown...as time expired, of course. I dreamed of meeting Jerry Rice, spending time with him, and playing football with him. You get the point—I idolized him.

In all my dreams of being like him and meeting him, there was the reality that Jerry Rice was, well, Jerry Rice. I was just a scrawny little third grader who had no access to the best NFL receiver of all time. If I tried hard, I might have been able to briefly meet him, but Drew and Jerry were never going to be best buds. We would never spend evenings playing football or hanging out…

Now imagine, after a long, grueling day in third grade, I received a phone call.

"Hello."

"Hey Drew, this is Jerry. How's it going?"

"Jerry who?"

"Jerry Rice. From the 49ers. The greatest wide receiver of all times. You know, number 8-0. I was wondering if we could hang out, like, all the time. I just think you're a cool guy, and I want to be your bud. I'd also like to personally train you to be the NFL's second greatest receiver of all time."

Of course, it would take a lot to convince me it was Jerry Rice, but if he showed up at my door to make good on his statement, I would be absolutely blown away. Blown away. Jerry Rice, eager to spend time with me! Willing to train me! Promising to help me get to the NFL! Here! With me! Jerry Rice, the G.O.A.T.! Blown away! My interaction with Jerry Rice would change the way I lived moment by moment. Not only would I improve my football skills, but I'd also have constant confidence in the fact that I had all-the-time access to Jerry Rice.

This analogy is just a whiff of what it would be like for the early Christians to hear "God's Spirit dwells in you" (1 Cor. 3:16). The promise of the Holy Spirit is shockingly extraordinary and changes everything. The incredible access to God' presence isn't just for a few first-century Christians; it's for all who believe. It's for you. "When you believed in Christ, he identified you as his own by giving you the Holy Spirit, whom he promised long ago. The Spirit is God's guarantee that he will give us the inheritance he promised and that he has purchased us to be his own people. He did this so we would praise and glorify him." (Eph. 1:13-14)

This is a glorious guarantee, a Jerry Rice showing up at your door moment, and this reality should move you to excitement and action. If all I did with Jerry Rice is welcome him in and then have him sit on the couch all his life, I would miss out on so much. In a way, I'd miss out on Jerry Rice. In the same way, if the promise of the Holy Spirit doesn't move you to a life of fully living out your faith, you are missing out.

One of the primary ways to engage with the Holy Spirit's power is by using your spiritual gifts. Spiritual gifts are special abilities God gives believers, through the Holy Spirit, to build His Kingdom. Spiritual gifts are sometimes supernatural, but most are human talents and passions, used in conjunction with the Holy Spirit to do God's work. By allowing the Holy Spirit to use you to build God's Kingdom, you are participating in the "greater things" Jesus was talking about. By exercising your spiritual gifts, you will more fully experience the life you have been saved for, the Holy Spirit you've been given, and God's power through you.

How Do You Find Out What Your Spiritual Gifts Are?

Romans 12 says, "For by the grace given to me I say to everyone among you not to think of himself more highly than he ought to think, but to think with sober judgment, each according to the measure of faith that God has assigned. For as in one body we have many members, and the members do not all have the same function, so we, though many, are one body in Christ, and individually members one of another. Having gifts that differ according to the grace given to us, let us use them: if prophecy, in proportion to our faith; if service, in our serving; the one who teaches, in his teaching; the one who exhorts, in his exhortation; the one who contributes, in generosity; the one who leads, with zeal; the one who does acts of mercy, with cheerfulness." (vv. 3-8 NIV)

Romans 12:6-8, First Corinthians 12:4-11, First Corinthians 12:27-31, and Ephesians 4:11 mention twenty-one different spiritual gifts. Some of the gifts are supernatural: healing, miracles, prophecies about the future, and speaking in tongues. Most of the gifts mentioned are not supernatural at their core but become supernatural by combining God-given talents with the Holy Spirit's direction and infusion (giving, mercy, teaching, etc.). Some theologians believe the twenty-one gifts are a complete catalog of all the gifts. I think the gifts mentioned are a sampling of a much broader reality of God's partnership with you. There are three reasons for this view.

First, some of the gifts mentioned are things all believers should participate in. If the lists given are a closed group, then it would be easy to think, "I don't have the gift of mercy, so I don't really need to be merciful." Well, that just isn't true. All believers are called to exercise mercy, but some believers have been given an extra dose of mercy to express the fuller picture of God's redeeming love.

Second, each time the gifts are mentioned, the authors give lists of differing lengths and differing gifts. No two lists are the same. There are also some gifts alluded to in the Old Testament that expand the lists even further (see Ex. 31:1-5). If the gifts were a closed canon of exactly twenty-one gifts, there would be greater alignment between these lists.

Lastly, I believe that God has uniquely gifted you to use your natural talents in tandem with His Holy Spirit to make a Kingdom impact. When you use the skills and the circumstances God has placed you in to build His Kingdom, your talents become Spirit-filled, spiritual gifts.

Now, if your talent involves sin, be assured it isn't a spiritual gift. The Spirit will not partner with you in sin. Also, you can't just call something a spiritual gift because you prayed that God would be with you while you do it. Asking God to be with you while you work is a noble prayer and something you should always do, but a spiritual gift moves beyond merely thinking about Jesus as you do it. Being good at your job is a talent. If you use your job to influence, encourage, and love others toward Christ, your work becomes a spiritual gift.

Here is what an expanded understanding of spiritual gifts might look like. A friend of mine used to play World of Warcraft. I'm not very familiar with the game, but it's a multiplayer, online game where you interact with people throughout the world. My friend enjoyed the game and was good at it (talent), but he didn't just play the game because it was fun; he played it with intention. I'm not sure how, but my friend held Bible studies and prayed for people all within the game. (Spirit directed and infused) His talent in the game allowed him to connect with others, enjoy what he was doing, use it to bring God glory, showing others God's love.

In this case, video games are part of his spiritual gifts because he allowed God's work to be done through his talent and enjoyment. After reading through the labels of spiritual gifts in the Bible, you may think my friend's spiritual gifts are evangelism and teaching, not video games. While I wouldn't disagree, when gifts are categorized within the traditional lists, it may be hard to connect how God wants to use your current situation to build His Kingdom. Starting with labels of "evangelism and teaching" and asking, "How can I implement those in my life?" can sometimes be a difficult connection to make. First, ask, "What talents and interests has God given me, and how can I use them to bring God glory?"

Another example is an auto mechanic I know who uses his talents and resources to bless those in need. He regularly shows the love and mercy of Jesus by fixing cars for free or significantly discounted. You won't find "auto mechanic" under the list of spiritual gifts, but his talent, guided by Jesus, infused with God's abundant mercy, is part of the "spiritual gift" package.

Starting with the Biblical lists is helpful for some, but in my experience, beginning with your natural talents tends to unveil the opportunities God has placed all around you to glorify Him. By expanding your understanding, I pray you will see the many possibilities to partner with God, to use your spiritual gifts.*

*Don't confuse spiritual gifts with the fruit of the Spirit. There are character traits, attitudes, and actions produced in all believers through the Holy Spirit. Spiritual gifts are more unique to the individual. Fruit of the Spirit should be growing in each person who believes—love, joy, peace, patience, kindness, gentleness, goodness, self-control. (see Gal. 5:22-23) The fruit of the Spirit is the by-product of a life lived in submission to the Spirit. They are character qualities that are developed in you to reveal the Spirit's work in your life, while spiritual gifts are outward actions used to serve and build up others toward Christ.

How Do I Start?
Prayer

Spend time asking God to make clear where He has gifted you. As you pray for clarity on your gifting, pray that God will provide opportunities to use your circumstances and talents to make a more significant impact for His Kingdom.

Perhaps you're handy with tools—with a little tinkering, you can fix almost anything. Well then, ask God to give you an opportunity to help someone out, assist a neighbor in need, or work on fixing something at church. Maybe you're a stay-at-home parent, and as you pray for clarity of your gifts, you get a sense that one of your spiritual gifts might be service. Use this awareness to pray that you will see some of your frustrations with your kids as opportunities to serve them and show them God's love. If you manage people, pray that God's Spirit will guide you in your interactions with those you oversee. Pray that the Holy Spirit will help you create opportunities to direct conversations in ways that show deep, Godly love to your employees.

Your prayers should not only focus on figuring out your gifts; they should include asking for the Holy Spirit's empowerment to make a God-glorifying impact in the work/hobbies/community you're already a part of. So, don't just pray for understanding. Pray for an opportunity.

Test

You can take many online tests to help you begin to discover what your spiritual gifts may be. These tests can provide you insights into areas of interest and ministry

> *Don't just pray for understanding. Pray for an opportunity.*

that you may not have seen before. I've found online tests to be somewhat helpful in giving direction. Because online tests limit their framework to a certain number of labels, they tend to focus on the traditional ways the listed gifts operate and not on how your natural passions and talents can be Spirit infused opportunities to build others up and bring God glory. Tests will limit your results to the gifts mentioned in the Bible, which may make it hard for you to see how you can partner with the Holy Spirit in everything you do.

I encourage you to take a few assessments and see if there is any alignment in your results. Then spend time engaging in the next three practices to seek confirmation and clarity as to what your spiritual gifts are. Here are a few online tests to begin.

https://gifts.churchgrowth.org/spiritual-gifts-survey/

https://spiritualgiftstest.com

https://giftstest.com

Put Into Practice

The best way to find your spiritual gifts is by committedly trying them out. Your church is a great place to start. If you think you are a person who can make others feel immediately welcomed and loved, commit to being part of the welcome team. If you think God has given you the patience to hang out with students, stop thinking about it and start acting on it.

There is a critical distinguishing word here that I don't want you to miss: 'committedly.' I guarantee you will experience tension, discomfort, or apathy when you start volunteering. If you don't commit to giving it your best effort and giving it a reasonable amount of time, these feelings can move you to an assumption that it is not your gift. Don't give in to that assumption quite yet. It may be accurate, but it may just be you need more time to get past those early jitters. Just because it's your spiritual gift doesn't mean things will be pain-free and comfortable. If it is a spiritual gift, there should be times where you have a sense of passion, compassion, and partnering with God.

Sometimes we discover our spiritual gifts by accident. If you're not sure of your gifts, start by exploring areas in which you are interested. Invest yourself in ministries of interest to see if you get a sense of the Spirit's empowerment and joy. This does not mean you will be graced with a deep sense of God's presence 100% of the time. But, in my experience, there will be a sense that God is working through you, and you will find some joy in it.

If you try something and find yourself dreading and hating it, then that probably isn't your gift, and that's okay. Try something else. Continue to invest yourself in the work of God's Kingdom until you find your gift. Then, with the power of the Holy Spirit, get after it. Depend on God's strength and allow Him to use you to build others up. Expose the world to His truth and love and show others how great it is to live out your spiritual gifts.

Seek Advice

Make sure you have people in your life who can give you advice. You can ask someone you know to take a spiritual gift test on your behalf to see what they see in you. It may be beneficial to each take the same test (about you) and then compare the results to see where you align and diverge. Ask a friend what she thinks your gifts are. Have her help you process your "test, prayer, and put into practice" journey to assist you in discovering your gifts. Have her observe you trying different spiritual gifts to give you feedback. (For example, if you think you're a welcoming person and they notice whenever you greet people, you have an annoyed look on your face, it would be good to know, and probably reveals that's not your gift.)

Having a friend to process this with can be a tremendous help in discovering your gifts, putting them into practice, and holding you accountable to keep seeking God's strength. We all need encouragement to fight the good fight. Even when you find "your thing," you'll need someone who will continue to pray for you and cheer you on.

Unwrap And Use Your Gifts

Christmas morning is always an exciting time for our kids to open, enjoy, and immediately use their gifts. My wife and I love picking out what we think will bring the kids the most happiness. It would be devastating if any wrapped presents were sitting under a very dead Christmas tree in July. It would mean that our kids missed out on the joy of what we gave and never fully experienced the Christmas we planned for them. God has given you spiritual gifts to build His Kingdom, to grow you, to be a light to the dark world, and for you to enjoy. Have you opened your gift? Have you used your gift? There is a life that God is eager for you to experience. As long as the gift sits unwrapped, you'll be missing out. So... open it, appreciate it, and share it with others!

<u>Questions For Reflection:</u>

- Do you know what your spiritual gifts are? If so, how have you put them to use? If not, what are some talents that you have that God might want to use to bring Himself glory?

- Whether a new concept or not—how does your perspective change knowing that God's Spirit dwells inside of you and He wants to empower you to do "even greater things"?

- How do you think your community and the world would be different if Christians engaged in their spiritual gifts?

- Who is someone you see and think, "God is using them"? What is it about their lives that makes you think that?

- What did your spiritual gifts tests reveal about you? Was there anything surprising?

- What do you need to involve yourself in to see if your assumed gifts are your actual gifts?

- Who can you seek advice from when it comes to Spiritual gifts?

Chapter 19

Discipleship...Mentorship

Nathan sat across from me, patiently listening to all I had to say as I sought his advice on what decision to make. The church had recently presented me with the opportunity to stay in Middle School ministry or launch a brand-new college/young adults' group. I shared with him all my fears of beginning something from scratch, my current tensions in my ministry, and my future hopes. I had no idea what to do, but I was leaning toward staying in the position I was already overseeing. He asked if there had been any clear direction from God, what my wife thought, and navigated the pros and cons of each option with me.

I trusted Nathan was in prayerful consideration and leaning on God's wisdom in his advice. After some time, he said, "Drew, can I just share what I've noticed?" He had served with me in the Middle School ministry for a few years, and I was eager to hear what he had to say. "Yes, please," I begged. "Over the last few years, I've heard the tone in the way you correct middle schooler's change," Nathan said. "It used to be a lighthearted, loving reprimand. Now there is a tone of frustration and impatience."

This single statement changed the trajectory of my thoughts, and ultimately the trajectory of my life. His investment in me, his discipleship of me, in tune with God's directing, brought light into an area I hadn't seen and made me realize it was time for me to move to the next opportunity. Discipleship is crucial for your walk with God—both for you and from you.

To Become A Pupil

The Greek word for disciple is "mathēteuō, meaning; to become a pupil; to enroll as a scholar,[1] but being a disciple of Christ means more than an intellectual assent of knowledge. It means learning from God, and then helping others study, understand, and follow Him. It means taking the "food" you've received and feeding others. I once heard someone put it this way, "You aren't a disciple until your disciples are making disciples." The responsibility of making disciples isn't reserved for the pastor or the "church organization." It is a responsibility for everyone who follows Christ. Every Christ-follower is called to intentionally invest in others' lives to help them develop into pupils of Jesus... who then develop others into pupils of Jesus.

Unfortunately, the calling and opportunity to disciple is often seen as the responsibility of church programs. Don't get me wrong, church programs are helpful in discipling people, BUT that should

> *Church programs are helpful in discipling people, BUT that should not be, and cannot be, the primary format of discipleship.*

not be, and cannot be, the primary format of discipleship. Relying on a church program to disciple others can easily place you back into the trap of becoming a passive observer. "If the church program does the discipling, then I can just point people there." This mindset silences your calling, limits your opportunity to grow, and constrains the church body's opportunity to impact more lives.

On top of that, the needs of the people in the church are always more extensive than a church program. If you're waiting for a church program that has access to every person's spiritual journey, knows each person's personality, and partners them with their ideal mentor, you'll be waiting forever. If instead, each person in the church took it upon themselves to ask, "Who has God placed in my life that I can disciple?" then we, the Church, might actually be able to respond to all the needs for spiritual guidance. Hopefully, you're convinced of your responsibility to make disciples, realizing you need to move from merely receiving to joyfully distributing what God has taught you.

I Don't Have What It Takes

Before you dismiss yourself from disciplining others, let me encourage you with two things. First, listen to the reminder Peter gives in First Peter 2:4-5 "As you come to him, the living Stone— rejected by humans but chosen by God and precious to him— you also, like living stones, are being built into a spiritual house to be a holy priesthood, offering spiritual sacrifices acceptable to God through Jesus Christ." (NIV)

What Peter is telling his readers has significant implications for you. You are part of a royal priesthood. You have direct access to God. (Remember the previous chapter—God's presence was something that was reserved for only the High Priest.) Peter's statement is remarkable. The power of God resides in every person who gives

their life to Christ! Like spiritual gifts, the ability to accomplish anything of eternal value comes from the Holy Spirit. In other words,
you may feel inadequate to disciple someone, but you must remember the Holy Spirit is with you and working through you.

Do you think, "I don't have
what it takes?" Be encouraged: YOU
DON'T, and yet YOU DO. On your
own, with your own strength and
ability, you don't have what it takes
to help people develop their relationship with God. But because you have
God's Spirit in you, He will work

> *Feeling unqualified
> is precisely what you
> should feel because
> that inadequacy
> should make you
> depend on God.*

through you (you do have what it takes). Feeling unqualified is precisely what you should feel because your inadequacy should make
you dependent on God. Don't allow the feeling of inadequacy to
stop you from doing what you've been called to do. Remember,
Jesus ends His command with "I will be with you to the very end
of the age." He doesn't call you to disciple others only to abandon
you with "bon voyage, and good luck with that." He journeys with
you. As long as you depend on Him, He provides the wisdom and
strength you need. He works with you and guides you as you guide
others. So be encouraged; you don't have what it takes, but you do
have what it takes.

I also want to remind you that you've got something in your
hand, right now, to disciple others. This book is focused on giving
you the tools to fully live out your faith. In other words, you have
a significant opportunity with the very thing you're reading to help
others develop their faith.

As you process all you've read, take others through this material. Use this book to help guide you through discipling others. This
book was written with two people in mind: you and the people you

will disciple. So don't fret; you've got a tool right here to help guide your discipleship.

Changing The Wording

Although I've already spent a good chunk of time using the word "discipleship," I'd like to change the wording to something most people have an easier time comprehending. In my experience, when the word "discipleship" or "discipling" is used, there tends to be two main reactions, dismissal and confusion. For some reason, discipling is seen as a task only the most mature Christians engage in. As we just discussed, this isn't true, but there is something about the word "discipleship" that makes people reluctant to engage. Confusion also comes from not understanding what discipleship means.

I've found there is much more receptivity to the idea of "mentorship." Not only is mentorship better understood, but it is also something many people desire. God-dependent mentorship is discipleship, but the word "mentorship" tends to be clearer for many. So, from here on out, I'll use the word "mentorship," but one more clarification needs to be made. Mentorship is God-focused, faith-encouraging, growth-inducing guidance, not just "life advice." With that definition, let's take a quick look at how to be mentored and how to mentor others.

I Want To Be Mentored

If you are seeking mentorship, GREAT! I believe that everyone, yes everyone, should have a mentor. Your desire to be mentored shows a willingness to

> *Mentorship is God-focused, faith-encouraging, growth-inducing guidance, not just "life advice."*

learn and grow, which is excellent. Here are three quick pieces of advice if you desire mentorship. (If you don't want mentorship, I encourage you to figure out why you wouldn't want someone to help guide you toward Christ-likeness. As you figure that out, pray against, and work to change your hesitancy)

1. Wanting a mentor doesn't preclude mentoring someone else. Don't fall into the trap of consuming and not exercising your faith, as we previously discussed. While you may be in a season when mentoring someone should wait, you don't have to wait to have a mentor to mentor someone else. I can almost guarantee you that as you mentor someone, you will grow too.

2. Reading this section will give you a great perspective on what you may want from a mentor and help you clarify, with your mentor, what you would like from your time together. So, as you read about "How to mentor," take notes on how you would want to be mentored.

3. ASK. Don't wait for someone to say, "Would you like a mentor?" Find someone who is more spiritually mature than you, someone you see living the life you want and ask them to mentor you. If they say they can't, keep searching until you find someone willing. Don't give up, and don't stay silent. Again, the value of a mentor is immense, so keep pursuing godly people to mentor you.

<u>Questions For Reflection:</u>

- Do you want to be mentored? What is keeping you from it?

- Who do you see in your life that can be a mentor? What is it about them that makes them "mentor" material?

- What would it take for you to ask to be mentored, and what would you want mentorship to look like?

Chapter 20

Moving Toward Mentoring

Input Before Output (Integrity)

To properly mentor others, you need to seek God and look to Him to lead you. In John 15, Jesus reminds His followers that God is the vine, and they are the branches. In order to produce good fruit, disciples (mentors) must be connected to the vine. It is foolish to think you can mentor people if you aren't regularly connecting to God. Connecting with God should produce a life of obedience to Him.

Granted, you will mess up, there will be times where you don't live up to what you've mentored someone else to do, but integrity is a significant part of mentorship. When you screw up, make sure you have someone you can talk with, confess to, and who will help you live more like Christ. There are few things more frustrating to God than spiritual hypocrisy (check out all the stories about Jesus and the religious leaders).

If you are mentoring someone and are not living the advice you are giving, you are not abiding in the vine. Abiding in God, seeking Him daily, and accountability are all things that need to be in your life to ensure you are leading with integrity. Integrity not only makes sure you live what you teach, but it also challenges you with the advice and questions you ask those you mentor. What I mean is that as you mentor others, in a way, you should be mentoring yourself.

You should evaluate your own life against the actions and attitudes you advise. There have been plenty of times I've counseled people regarding how God might be directing them, only to have the Holy Spirit convict me of not acting the way I advised.

> *Abiding in God, seeking Him daily, and account- ability are all things that need to be in your life to ensure you are leading with integrity.*

Because integrity is so crucial to mentorship, these circumstances have pushed me to respond to the Spirit's conviction and align my life with the counsel I gave to the person I mentored. Just recently, I advised someone in their relationship with their spouse. I gave some solid, godly correction on how he was treating his spouse, only to head home from work and treat my wife in the selfish way I had spoken against. The Holy Spirit quickly convicted me of my attitude and my lack of integrity. I had to respond to the very words the Holy Spirit spoke through me to the person I was mentoring and apologize to my wife.

Mentoring someone takes a high level of integrity, and integrity benefits your walk with God because it's a mirror to the guidance you give and the life you live.

Get To Know People

To mentor someone, you first have to get to know them, showing you care for them. Unless there is a foundation for your relationship, it is very challenging to make mentorship work. An old adage says, "People don't care how much you know until they know how much you care," and this statement is oh so true in mentorship. Standing in a church lobby and tapping someone on the shoulder, asking, "Would you like me to mentor you?" will rarely, if ever, be well received. Finding opportunities to know others prior to mentorship shows that you genuinely care about pouring into them and gives you a chance to show you are a loving, intentional, approachable person. In a way, it helps you practice mentorship by deeply listening and caring for those you are getting to know, without the commitment. Caring for others outside of a mentorship relationship also builds trust, making the mentorship foundation stronger.

Lastly, it helps you get to know potential mentees in a way that may save you from much bigger frustrations further down the road. Not all mentors and mentees work well together. Whether it's interests, personality, or time, sometimes a mentor and a mentee just don't connect. Getting to know people outside of the mentorship relationship may allow you to spot reasons you may not want to mentor them (and vice versa).

As you build relationships, be sure to enter "people places" with prayer. Before you go to work, school, church, or social gatherings, be praying that God will give you an opportunity to care for someone, to listen to them, and to get to know them. Ask Him to grant you the ability to develop a deeper relationship that points to Christ. I believe that God is setting up connections with others all the time, but we often miss them because we're not listening or are too busy with our own agendas.

Pray

As you get to know people pray that God will reveal to you who you should mentor. Pray for the heart of the person or people you will mentor, asking God to help them grow, and relying on Him for the wisdom you will offer. Pray that God will use you and grow you too. Ask God, if there is a specific person He wants you to mentor, that he or she will be receptive to mentorship (or even ask for it). Prepare your heart, in prayer, both before starting and throughout your mentorship.

Invite To Hang Out/Mentor

Asking someone if they are interested in mentorship doesn't have to be as awkward as you may think. "I see something in you that you need help with, and I have the answer to your need" is not the way to start the conversation. Please don't say anything like that, and please don't walk up to someone and say, "God told me to mentor you." (Unless He clearly did, AND He told you to tell them.) If God has made it clear to you, then here are some better ways to approach someone you'd like to mentor.

"I've been praying about pouring into the life of someone, and God has connected us. I'm wondering if you'd be interested in meeting regularly to talk about life and God?"

"God has been challenging me to use my faith to encourage someone in their faith, and you came to mind. Would you like to get together regularly so I can encourage you in your faith?"

"I'd like to be able to use what God has been teaching me to build up and share with others. What do you think about getting together every couple of weeks to talk about life and faith?"

Still, even these may seem a little forced, so why not pray that God provides a more natural avenue of connecting? Then, look for opportunities to dive deeper. Perhaps the person you are praying about mentoring tells you of a need or prayer request. How about offering to help solve the need, committing to praying for the request, and checking back in regularly? Perhaps the person begins to share some struggles he has. Why not invite a more in-depth conversation over coffee? Or, it could be as easy as saying, "Hey, would you like to grab lunch sometime so we can get to know each other better and I can hear more about what God is doing in your life?"

Whichever the case, use this time to hear where he is in his relationship with God. Listen carefully, ask the Spirit to guide your questions, and pray for him. When you're done meeting, make sure you let him know that you enjoyed your time and would like to do it more often, if he'd like. There may be a rare time where someone comes up to you and asks, "Will you mentor me?" I've found that most mentoring relationships are established by the mentor (you) pursuing an intentional relationship with the mentee. Don't be scared away from mentoring by the false idea that "if God wants me to mentor someone, it will just happen…naturally." There are always opportunities to mentor others in the church community (children, youth, young adults, young married, new to faith, etc.). It will take you working, not waiting, for it to happen.

Mentorship doesn't happen without relationships and asking someone to spend time with you to grow a friendship and grow their relationship with God—who doesn't want that?... Well, some people may not want that. If your offer gets rejected, don't be afraid to ask why not (not argumentatively, but full of a desire to understand). You may find that the reason has nothing to do with you, and you can continue to pray for the person, leaving an opportunity open for the future.

> *Don't be scared away from mentoring by the false idea that "if God wants me to mentor someone, it will just happen…naturally."*

Or, you may find out something harsh about yourself and why they don't want YOU. Yeah, that will sting, but it could also reveal something you may need to change about your character, to help you become someone others desire mentorship from.

Questions For Reflection:

- What scares you most about being a mentor? Why do you think that is?

- Have you ever been mentored? Was it helpful? What was most beneficial?

- If you had to list the reasons you don't want to/can't mentor others, what would your top two excuses be?

- On a scale of 0-10 ("0" meaning no integrity to "10" full of integrity), how would you rank your integrity? Why that number?

- In what areas of your life, specifically, do you need to move up your integrity number?

- How can you surround yourself with a mentor to increase your integrity? Name that person and write down what you need to talk to them about…then do it.

- Who has God surrounded you with that you need to be intentional in getting to know?

- How can you "practice mentorship" this week?

- Spend time praying about what God wants you to do and who God might want you to mentor.

Chapter 21

How To Mentor

The book series "For Dummies" is widely popular, and some of its most astonishing titles are: *Green Smoothies for Dummies, Acne for Dummies,* and no joke, *Retired Racing Greyhounds for Dummies.* These books take each subject and simplify information to easily communicate the ins-and-outs of the topic. Imagine this next section as *Mentoring for Dummies* (though there is an actual *Mentoring for Dummies book).* Now, I'm not calling you a dummy, but what I want to show you is, with these tools, mentoring is easy to accomplish…even a dummy can do it.

Just Do It

Mentoring definitely won't work if all you do is read about it and wait for something to happen. If you have decided to follow Christ, your calling is to make disciples. Jesus doesn't tell you to become an expert before you take action. He gives you an expert to work with—His Holy Spirit. If Christ has made a difference in your life, you need to respond in a way that makes a difference in others' lives. The gifts you've been given are to be used to bless and grow others. Yes, it can be scary. Yes, it can be awkward, but you have been called to do it, and the joy of following Jesus and having Him use you to impact others' lives FAR outweighs any reason not to.

Pray

I know I've already talked about the importance of prayer, so let me remind you of Paul's challenge to "pray without ceasing" (First Thess. 5:17, ESV). The responsibility of mentoring someone should elevate your desperate need for God through prayer. While you meet, pray that God gives you the words to say. While your mentee is sharing, ask God to help you know what you need to respond to. Ask God to make you bold when you need to be, to rebuke when you need to, and to encourage when you need to. Ask Him to bring to mind Bible verses or stories which guide each of these areas. Pray you won't advise out of human wisdom, but that God will give you His wisdom.

Remember, this relationship is not primarily about providing good life advice or giving your mentee a sounding board. Both of those things are good, but the primary purpose is to help him or her become more like Christ and take steps to abide deeply in God's love. For this to happen, the Holy Spirit must be at work. This means you must be continually relying on Him to work in and through you

> *The primary purpose of mentorship is to help others become more like Christ and take steps to abide deeply in God's love.*

and your mentee. Before the meeting, and as you meet, be praying without ceasing for God's guidance.

Clarify

In high school, when a flirty friendship moved to hanging out more exclusively, friends of the "couple" would always ask, "Have you had a 'DTR'?" DTR stands for "Define the relationship." The DTR is a conversation to clarify the relationship. Boyfriend/girlfriend? Just friends? Interested in dating, but not yet boyfriend and girlfriend? The DTR allows both people to know the relationship's intention so they can interact with one another with understanding. A DTR in a mentor/mentee relationship is helpful for the same reasons. It clarifies the expectations of the mentorship interaction.

One of the most significant tensions I've seen in mentoring is a mismatched expectation of what mentorship is. One person has an idea of what they would like from their time together, and the other person has a very (or even slightly) different expectation, creating dissension and discouragement from both parties. This disconnect usually ends up with the relationship disintegrating, and both feeling like mentorship just didn't work out. Granted, there are times when personalities, schedules, and desires don't align (we'll deal with that later), but I've found that most often the mentorship relationship breaks down because of the assumed roles and expectations of each person. This problem would be quickly eliminated if there was a DTR.

How to Have a DTR

You may think these conversations are going to be awkward and feel unnatural. I mean, when is the last time you talked to your friend about the expectations of your relationship? Your fear can be silenced because it doesn't have to be weird or forced at all. Here are some ways to naturally have that conversation.

The easiest time to have the conversation is when someone asks you to mentor them. The person pursuing mentorship probably has some sort of expectation, which is why they are asking you. Set up a time to meet and have them come ready to answer: What do they want from mentorship? How often would they like to meet? In what areas do they desire to grow?

Setting up a later meeting will allow them to process what they want and show you their commitment level. If they forget about the meeting, show up late, or come unprepared to answer the questions, it could reveal they may not be as committed or invested as you'd hope. It may mean you adjust your expectations or clearly define your expectations of investment.

If you have pursued someone to mentor, you'll want to answer the same expectation questions and talk about what you were thinking the mentorship could look like. This should happen as early as possible because it establishes clarity for moving forward. Whenever you have the DTR, it should be done humbly and be motivated out of love, not out of a sense of superiority. You should share your heart for growing and seeing them grow. A great way to approach the DTR is with the foundation of Proverbs 27:17.

"Iron sharpens iron, so a friend sharpens a friend."

This verse points to a mutually strengthening reality. It sets an expectation that meeting together is going to grow both of you. Although you are the mentor, never forget that God can use your mentee to grow you. In fact, you should expect it. After you've shared your heart for them, for God, for growth, ask them if they'd like to meet regularly to build one another up.

Whether you were asked to mentor, or you asked someone if you could pour into their life, you'll want to continue to clarify what your time together looks like. Below are different ways in which mentorship can be approached. Use them to guide your expectations.

Options For Mentorship

As we go through these options, know they are not mutually exclusive; mentorship can focus on one, a few, or all of these areas. While you may choose to focus on one, naturally, the other focuses should find themselves in your conversations. Whichever approach you use, never forget the primary goal of becoming more like Christ.

Bible Study

Your mentorship could be a study of a book or books of the Bible. If this is the focus, set expectations for what you will be reading between one meeting and the next. Agree on what you will come prepared to discuss. I'd encourage you to practice S.O.A.P.ing, as well as writing down any areas of confusion in the passage. This way, when you meet, there will be some directives in sharing. There are a ton of resources—books, videos, online guides—that can help you process the reading and your conversations. If you choose to not use pre-created resources, here are some questions to help stoke conversations with your mentee:

Any areas of confusion? Questions?

What stood out to you? Why might God have been drawing your attention to that?

What did your reading reveal about God? About you?

How has your reading enhanced or challenged your relationship with God? With others?

Be sure you come ready to answer the questions as well—remember more is caught than taught. A mentor who doesn't practice what he preaches is not full of integrity.

Topical Study

Your mentee may be interested in studying a specific Biblical or character topic. God's grace, leadership, marriage, lust, or anger are just a few issues that can be explored. Again, there are a ton of resources to help you discover the depths of these subjects. Just like a Bible study, setting expectations of what you will read or watch between meetings is crucial.

When you meet, ask your mentee what they've learned, share what you've learned, and spend time asking questions about how the knowledge gained can be put into action. Remember what your mentee shared and check in with him to make sure that he is taking action on

> *It is entirely okay to say, "I don't know a lot about that," as long as it's accompanied by, "but let's learn together.".*

those items. You don't have to be an expert on the subject to be a successful mentor. You just have to have a willingness to co-explore. It is entirely okay to say, "I don't know a lot about that," as long as it's accompanied by, "but let's learn together."

Accountability

Accountability is an incredible thing that is often seen as the opposite: awkward and unwanted. Unfortunately, in our "don't judge culture," many Christians have bought into the lie that we are to accept each other without any responsibility to correct sin. That is not true. Most of the New Testament is a commentary on behavior that should be reformed in believer's lives. Yes, the grace of God covers our sins, and He invites everyone to come to Him as they are, but when we accept Jesus as our Savior, there is a clear expectation we will model our lives after Him, in obedience to Him. "Take up the cross and follow me (Jesus)" (Mt. 16:24). Following Jesus isn't about staying in our sin, taking advantage of His love. It's about letting His love challenge and change us to move from anything that doesn't reflect Him. Jesus establishes His church with an inseparable responsibility to one another. The body of Christ is not just here to serve and worship God. He has put us together to challenge, encourage, and refine one another.

Accountability usually has one of two focuses: "away from" and "toward" an action or attitude. Examples of accountability "toward" include: Seeing God's blessing, interacting intentionally with co-workers, starting a prayer meeting at work, building a relationship with neighbors, and more. Accountability "away from" can include: Eliminating pornography, pride, gossip, anger, selfishness, greed, and more. Although "away from" has a different primary focus than "toward," both "away from" and "toward" have to practice the opposite in order to succeed. Here is what I mean. To move away from anger, you have to move toward love. To move away from pride, you need to move toward humility. To move toward a prayer meeting, you have to move away from your calendar being so busy. To move toward building a relationship with your neighbors, you have to move away from your comfort.

Both directions of accountability include the other, but the primary focus will usually be one or the other. As you mentor, keep in mind both types of accountability. After all, your goal is not just to help someone sin less; you want to help them become more like Christ.

Remember: In the spiritual disciplines chapter, I talked about not misusing the confessional time as simply "offloading." Accountability can fall into the same trap. If your accountability only means "I tell someone when I screwed up," and "I don't take any steps to move from the sin," then you aren't actually in an accountable relationship.

As a mentor, this is a very tough role to have. How do you hold someone accountable who is looking to you for guidance but doesn't seem to want to turn from their sin? The best approach is to lovingly call out what you see. (i.e. "Hey, you've asked me to hold you accountable for your anger toward your wife, but I've noticed you haven't taken any other steps to curb your anger. It doesn't seem like confessing to me is helping you move in the right direction. Why is that? How can we work together to make accountability actually help?") I know this is tough, but if you love your mentee, you will call out where he is messing up.

Tim Keller offers this helpful insight when it comes to confrontation, accountability, and sin:

Any love that is afraid to confront the beloved is not really love, but a selfish desire to be loved. This kind of selfish love is afraid to do what is right (toward God and the beloved) if it risks losing the beloved's affection. It makes an idol out of the beloved. It says, "I'll do anything to keep him or her loving me!" This is not loving the person. It is loving the love you get from the person. In other words, it is loving yourself more than the person. So, any "love" that cuts corners morally, or fails to confront, is not really love at all."[1]

As you participate in your loving challenge, work to figure out and implement a higher structure for accountability. (i.e., "How about I text you every other day to check in?" or "Schedule a reminder to ping every day when driving home to pray for your wife so when you see her your time is soaked in prayer.") These practices then become another avenue of accountability that help him move away from the action or attitude. Accountability only works if the person asking for it actually wants change and will be honest. You can't control others' actions, but you can be aware of when "accountability" is being used to ignore the change your mentee claims he wants.

Life Processing

Life processing is part of all mentorship. Mentoring someone without helping them connect what they are learning and how they are growing to their everyday life is purposeless. Whichever focus you pursue; you should always help your mentee see how God is working in and through them. This process shouldn't just be broad. Help tie what she is learning and seeing in her marriage, school, work, family, service to others, to what God wants from her and for her. Connecting the discussion to her life is crucial for her growth and vital for developing your mentoring relationship.

While processing life is a healthy part of all mentorship, it can be the primary focus of your time together too. My previous mentor and I met every other week, ate dinner, and simply talked about life. We shared the ups and downs of the last few weeks, talking about our families and work. We asked each other questions about why we were frustrated or thrilled about certain things. We'd exchanged advice on how to handle tensions, and our meetings always ended by answering this one question: How have you seen God in the last two weeks?

Our mentorship was built on a deep friendship that produced a desire to care for one another and help each other process life and point to Jesus. Even though there was only one question that we committed to asking each time, I was being mentored throughout our conversations. My mentor was a good listener, a good questioner, and someone who was in tune with God. We didn't have an agenda to work through, but the value of having someone who loved God, loved and listened to me, and listened to God for me, had a massive impact on my life and was genuinely life changing.

You may feel this form of mentorship is not structured enough. My experience (in both mentoring and being mentored) has proved this type of mentorship is immensely helpful...as long as the mentor does these three things: Asks good questions, listens well, and, most important, responds dependent on the Holy Spirit. If these things aren't done, then the mentor is just a sounding board and an advice-giver (which isn't necessarily bad, but it misses out on the fullness of spiritual mentorship).

As a mentor, you want to listen to God's voice for your mentee. By asking good questions, you can work past the shallows of easy answers into deep soul exploration. By listening well, you show a depth of care that builds trust. By relying on the Holy Spirit, you can be confident you are mentoring toward Christ and not just toward "good ideas." Like I said before, rely on the Holy Spirit by praying without ceasing before and during your meetings. As your mentee shares, ask the Lord to give you wisdom in how to respond.

> *As a mentor, you want to listen to God's voice for your mentee.*

DO NOT MENTOR SOMEONE OF THE OPPOSITE SEX:

There are three main reasons for this.

1. There are usually issues each gender goes through (temptations, frustrations, and emotions) that could make sharing difficult. A mentor of the opposite sex might have a hard time understanding some of these. Being mentored by the opposite sex limits the opportunity to grow in these areas.

2. Mentorship exposes you to emotions and vulnerability that can easily lead to connecting with each other in an unsafe way (especially married people—but even unmarried can enter into a mentoring relationship that may have one

person's heart being tied to the other person in an undesired way.) I say this as someone who has mentored the opposite sex. I always made sure meetings were in public places with a lot of people around, and my wife knew when these meetings occurred. Even with all those safety precautions, I've realized mentoring the opposite sex put both them and me in an unnecessarily vulnerable space. Mentorship will likely deal with personal issues and hardships, exposing each person to emotional connections which could be easily avoided if you just allowed someone else to take on the role of the mentor. This doesn't mean you don't offer advice or listen to the needs and counsel someone of the opposite sex (Well, for some of you, it does). It does mean you shouldn't place yourself in a mentor relationship with the opposite sex.

3. There are plenty of women who can mentor women and plenty of men who can mentor men. If you think you have to be the one to mentor someone of the opposite sex, you're eliminating the opportunity for someone of the same sex to mentor that person. On top of that, you may have an ego problem, believing that you are the exception to the previous risks.

Questions For Reflection:

- Of the mentoring options—Bible study, topic, accountability, life processing—which do you think you'd be best at? Why?

- Which do you think you'd be the worst at? Why?

- Which would you like to be mentored in?

- What do you like about each different style of mentorship?

- What is keeping you from mentoring someone else?

Chapter 22

Making Your Mentorship Work

I'm sure you've seen those infomercials where some bad actor is hopelessly trying to figure out something, and the product he is selling makes the impossibly difficult task extraordinarily easy. One of my favorite commercials shows a man falling over, getting wrapped up in, and becoming horribly frustrated with his garden hose. I've used many hoses throughout my life and have yet to have one attack me and beat me down, but apparently, this is a common problem... until now. With this new hose, what was a life and death struggle can now be enjoyed for its true purpose: watering your flowers.

The irony of these infomercials is both the task they are presenting is never as complicated as they make it, and the product they are selling never makes it as easy as they claim. In this chapter, I want to help you realize the same about mentoring: It is not as difficult as you think, and yet, as helpful as these tools are, it still takes hard work to make it successful. So, here are some more tools to help make your mentoring work.

Be Consistent (Schedule it, Fight for it)

A successful mentorship relationship must have consistency and time. Jesus, the ultimate mentor, had his disciples live with Him 24/7 for three years. He taught them regularly. He traveled with them. He fed them. He deeply knew His guys. I'm not suggesting you have to have your mentee move in with you (But if God prompts you to… then you absolutely should have them move in). I am suggesting that mentorship will not be successful if it is inconsistent and time together is far apart. Not only does lack of consistency create a very difficult environment for relational growth, it limits growth opportunities for your mentee's life. Imagine if, as a kid, you only went to school six times a year. I know you would have thought that was awesome, but your growth in school would be a joke… You'd still be in kindergarten!

Your desire, as a mentor, is to help your mentee grow and to see her life becoming more Christ-like. Don't sabotage mentorship by having noble desires and believing significant growth can happen with inconsistent, infrequent meetings.

"But I'm Busy"

Our culture values busyness. When we aren't busy, mindless entertainment fills in the gaps. If the thought of consistently and frequently meeting with an individual overwhelms you, ask yourself these two questions: What did God call you to? And, are your busyness and entertainment more important than people?

This may sound harsh, but there is no "Go and make disciples…unless you work 80 hours a week and have kids in three different sports." While it may seem unreasonable to pour into others with the schedule you have, you must remember helping someone in their faith is considerably more important than so many other things that fill your life.

So, if you're busy, don't adjust how you respond to God; adjust how you react to the other requirements. If your work, sports, entertainment, or hobbies keep you from investing in others, then maybe you need to

> *Jesus does not say, "Go and make disciples... unless you work 80 hours a week and have kids in three different sports."*

evaluate which of those other things you need to remove or adjust. (And to be clear, your family is your first ministry. Make sure you're pouring into them.)

Be Intentional

"Be intentional" means being diligent to make sure your conversations and mentorship are moving toward Christ-likeness. This goes back to "Define the relationship." Answering "What is this for?" and "What do you want to move toward?" should direct what you talk about, what questions you ask, and where you press into things. An example might help.

If you're meeting with someone struggling in their marriage who wants to be a better spouse, it is fine to talk about work, sports, and what happened last weekend in the news. It is also great to talk about what they are reading for their quiet time and what insights they've gained, but if those topics are the only things discussed, you're missing the mark.

If the goal is to be a better spouse, make sure you ask questions about their interaction with their spouse in tandem with their relationship with God. Connect your advice, challenge, and encouragement to Christ-like character development as a husband/ wife/couple. You could take them out on a double date to model a healthy relationship. Intentionality means you aren't just getting together regularly and "shooting the breeze," but that, as a mentor, you are directing the conversations to help in the process of transformation.

Tip 1: DON'T back away from intentionally asking the hard questions. There will be times when you'll want to press into something your mentee brings up. Maybe the Holy Spirit is prompting you to ask the tough questions, but fear of how your mentee may react will try to silence you. Don't settle for comfort. (Don't force discomfort either.)

As a mentor, it is your responsibility to speak into your mentee's life, which won't always be easy. Let me reassure you, though: Some of the most significant breakthroughs I've seen have come when a mentor asks the tough questions or speaks the uncompromising truth, even though it would be easier not to. Don't give up on intentionality because of fear.

Tip 2: Care about more than just their issues. Don't sit down at your meeting and start firing questions at your mentee that only have to do with the areas he needs to grow. Care for all areas of his life, not just his problems. Talk about his interests, how his work is going, laugh together, enjoy each other's company. A good mentor is someone who deeply loves his mentee and knows about more than just his mentee's issues.

Give Space For Processing
(Ask A Lot Of Questions And Be Quiet)

Each person you mentor will differ—expect that. I've sometimes asked one question, and an hour later a mentee has verbally processed everything that has happened in his life over the last week.

I've mentored people who I've had to ask the same question four or five different ways, then sit in silence for two to three minutes as he internally processed his thoughts. I've mentored people who ask 15-minute questions. I've mentored people who always give a shallow first answer and have needed me to push further to get to deeper truth. All that to say—mentoring is a dance, and each partner is different.

The two most important skills for mentorship to be fruitful (outside of a dependence on God) are the ability to ask good questions and knowing when to be quiet. Please notice I didn't say, "the ability to give good advice." Yes, that is important, but if you can ask good questions and know when to be quiet, you'll be considerably more successful.

Asking good questions revolves around four things:

1. Genuine Care For Your Mentee

Good questions come from a heart that genuinely wants to know what is going on in your mentee's life. They come from a desire for your mentee to know Jesus more and experience the life He has created for her. If your mentorship is a task that you have to fulfill with a person you don't like, it doesn't matter how "good" your questions are...they won't be good.

2. Ask Questions In Multiple Ways

In their book *Made to Stick*, Chip and Dan Heath talk about the "curse of knowledge." Here is what they say. "When we know something, it becomes hard for us to imagine not knowing it. As a result, we become lousy communicators."[1] As a mentor, you've been placed in a position where you probably have more knowledge or life experience than your mentee. This experience is a good thing, but beware: it can lead you to believe the guidance you offer is obvious, easy, or straightforward. Your "curse of knowledge" can lead to a disconnect with your mentee if you don't work hard to understand her perspective and communicate in the way she needs. Asking a lot of questions will allow both you and your mentee to better understand her struggles and strengths. It will also fight the potential frustration which may come from what you think is a "simple question," a question which your mentee may have no idea how to handle.

I'll give an example in a second, but before I do, a quick warning: Don't make the opposite mistake and patronize your mentee. Instead, come to meetings praying that God will help you know how to ask the right questions, questions that will help your mentee think through things differently. When approached with grace and a desire to help her grow, multiple questions become a way to dig for a deeper response and greater understanding, not a repetitive interrogation.

Here is an example of a "curse of knowledge" question, followed by multiple ways of asking different questions to help your mentee answer the question.

How has God been speaking to you this week?

While this may seem simple, it may actually be a very tough question to answer. Your mentee could be thinking:

"Like audibly? I have never actually 'heard' God."

"Through someone else? My grandma was acting weird the other day when she talked to me...was that God?"

"How in the world does God actually 'speak'?"

To someone who has been around Christianity for a while, this is an "obvious and clear" question, but it may not be so obvious and clear to your mentee. Asking and reframing questions is an important skill in being a great mentor. So, here are multiple questions that gently uncover the answer to; "How has God been speaking to you this week?"

- What were the best parts of your week? Why were they so great? Why did you enjoy them so much?

- What do you think about the idea that God might be trying to communicate with you through your passions and experiences?

- If you gave a gift to someone you loved and you saw that they enjoyed the present, how would that make you feel and why?

- What would you hope your friend knew or remembered about YOU as they enjoyed the gift?

- James says, "Every good and perfect gift comes from above" (1:17, NIV). Why do you think God gifted you with your good experiences this week?

- When you think back to your highlights from this last week, as a gift from God, what might He be helping you understand about Him? About yourself?

As you can see, multiple questions allow your mentee to hear things from different angles, giving her a chance to answer easier questions, processing with you. Each of the answers she gives to these questions could also spur you to ask many other questions… and that's what we'll look at next.

3. Don't Settle For Easy Answers

Often, your mentee will answer your questions fairly quickly and expect to move on. Mentorship is not the place for quick answers and moving on. It's a place for reflection and soul searching. That doesn't happen by going through a checklist of questions and wrapping up your time. This means one of your primary jobs as a mentor is to help explore the answers your mentee gives, gently leading them to more in-depth pro-cessing. I do not mean you should interrogate them like a detective, frustrated with anything less than a full confession and crying. Instead, I suggest you prayerfully listen to what your mentee is talking about, paying attention to where your heart is stirred and pressing into their answers with questions or statements to probe deeper.

> *One of your primary jobs as a mentor is to help explore the answers your mentee gives, gently leading them to more in-depth processing.*

Here are some examples:

- "What do you mean by_____."

- "When you said you were really angry about that, why do you think that made you so angry? Does that have to be something which angers you so much? What would it take for _____ not to bother you so much? Does your anger have more to do with the situation or the person? Why is that?"

- "Why do you think you and your wife keep getting into arguments over ____? …But why does that particular thing set you two off? What would you need to have happen for that to not result in an argument? What's preventing you from taking those steps? What kind of discussions have you had about that issue outside your times of frustration?"

- "What makes your Bible reading so difficult? What have you tried/not tried? Why not try_____?"

- "What keeps you from having that conversation with your friend? Why do you think she will react negatively? What is the worst outcome of a conversation? What is the best outcome? Why does the worst outweigh the best? Do you think the voice of 'the worst' is God's voice or the devil's? If the devil's, then what do you think you need to do to silence 'the worst' voice and rely on 'the best'?'"

- "You've said you want to eliminate this sin in your life, but you haven't taken any precautions/set anything in place to eliminate the opportunity. Why is that?...Yes, but why is that..."

- "You seem to be relying on your own strength to like your co-worker. What would it look like to rely more on Christ's strength? What can you do to seek and act on God's strength, not your own?"

- "I've heard the same frustration with your parents the last four times we've met. What can be done to move away from your anger? What are you doing to move you away from this continual frustration because doing nothing is going to get the same results as the last two months?"

Asking open-ended questions will help move your mentee beyond their first, obvious answers. "What does your co-worker do that makes you so frustrated?" is a close-ended question which may help identify the point of frustration, but "Why does your co-worker's action bother you so much?" is an open-ended question, requiring your mentee to reflect more profoundly.

Close-ended questions are a good starting point since they are easier to answer, but don't stop there. Close-ended questions usually can be responded to with "yes" or "no," or have a limited set of possible responses (i.e., Do you want to quit your job?). Open-ended questions tend to prompt answers in sentences, lists, or stories. (i.e., Why do you think you would like another job? What is it about leaving your job that interests you? What do you think God wants you to do? Why?)

As you can see, each open-ended question doesn't settle for just receiving information from your mentee; it challenges her to think deeper about her response. Your job as a mentor is to help her link her reflections to her relationship and reliance on God. Think about it this way—everything is spiritual and can be part of a conversation with God. How are you moving your mentorship from a conversation between you and your mentee to a conversation between you, your mentee, and God?

4. Be Quiet

Please, please, please remember that SILENCE IS OKAY... AND NECESSARY. Don't use your time as a platform to give an hour lecture about everything you know, even if the person you are mentoring is difficult to talk to. The benefit of asking a question and letting it linger is a good thing. Throughout your meeting, you may only ask a few questions, but silence, reflection, and internal dialogue may be doing much more than you think. If the silence gets too agonizingly long, here are two good questions: "What are you thinking? What's going on in your mind?"

Suppose your mentee seems to be shut down to any conversations. In that case, you can lovingly say, "It seems like you aren't really interested in talking about this. Is everything alright?" You can also offer an empathetic story from your life related to what you think they may be wrestling with. However they respond to your story or your questions, you may need to pause the conversation and offer to pray for them right then. If you've made a breakthrough in conversation, great. If not, feel free to move the discussion to another, lighter topic, showing you care for all of them, not just the issue you were dealing with.

As a general practice, keep in mind the "80-20 Rule" of conversations: You should only be talking, at most, 20% of the time, and you should, at a minimum, be actively listening 80% of the time. Each mentoring relationship is different, but this is a useful guidepost for healthy mentoring conversations.

Asking good questions takes practice. Don't assume your conversations will flow with ease because you've read these tips, but don't be discouraged either. Sometimes you will be stonewalled by the emotions or tensions your mentee is dealing with. Being present and showing your mentee you care for her is more valu-

> *You should only be talking, at most, 20% of the time, and you should, at a minimum, be actively listening 80% of the time.*

able than being the world's best question asker. Work hard to ask questions in multiple ways, don't settle for the easy answers, and be okay with silence. Above all these skills, make sure the questions are infused with genuine care for your mentee.

Make Your Mentoring More Than Just Meeting Time

Mentorship is built on trust, and trust is built on relationships. A valuable investment to your mentoring would be to develop your friendship outside of your "meeting time" or include "fun" as part of your regular meetings. This doesn't mean you have to hang out all the time, but it does mean you show your mentee you enjoy being around her. Have her over for dinner, attend a sporting event, go fishing, get a pedicure, go to the beach, go on vacation, have fun together somehow. Even doing this once or twice a year will go a long way to build trust and show your mentee truly care.

Sending your mentee a text is a little thing you can do to show you care. When you're praying for her, send a text to let her know. Maybe text and ask how her day is going or share something you heard which reminded you of her. The little opportunities to say, "I'm thinking about you outside of our meeting time," really build relational equity, which will lead to a more fruitful mentoring relationship.

Pray Together

Sitting in my office at church I attempted to conclude my meeting by asking the young lady that sat across from me, "Is there anything else?" She looked at me like I was crazy, and said, "Well... are we going to pray?" We ended our time in prayer. While I don't recall what we talked about, I will never forget the absurdity this person felt about meeting and not praying together. This interaction has been a constant reminder to have the same assumption. It would be crazy to talk about all of life's "stuff" and not spend dedicated time speaking directly to God. Even though praying out loud might terrify you, as a mentor, you need to fight through your fear. Praying together models prayer to your mentee, teaching him as he observes and listens to you speaking to God. Having your mentee listen to your prayers may heighten your nervousness, so please remember what we talked about in the prayer section. Prayer is about you talking with God. You don't need to have eloquent words. God already knows what you are going to say, so just talk to Him. Ultimately, you want your mentoring to help your mentee grow closer to Jesus.

Prayer reminds and reinforces dependence on God. If your mentee leaves your meeting with sound advice from you, that's fantastic, but he needs to know the guidance you are giving him is through the wisdom of the Holy Spirit and that wisdom is accessible to him as he grows in dependence on God. Mentoring is not about making your mentee believe he just needs to "try harder." It's about helping him know that he needs to "rely harder." Prayer is an engine toward a deeper reliance on God. So, pray for your mentee both inside and outside of your meeting time. Mentors have to be "pray-ers."

Follow Up

When you leave a mentor meeting, be sure you remember what you talked about. If you've got a great memory, be thankful. If you don't, write down some notes to help you remember. Your mentee won't feel cared for if she has to share, re-share,

> *If your mentee leaves your meeting with sound advice from you, that's fantastic, but he needs to know the guidance you are giving him is through the wisdom of the Holy Spirit and is accessible to him as he grows in dependence on God.*

and re-re-share the same stories of her life. On the other hand, a significant way to show you care is to follow up on the things you talked about in the previous meetings.

For example, if she shared she is having a problem with one of her parents, at the next meeting make sure to ask, "How are the frustrations with your parents?" Maybe, in a past meeting, she told you about a negative interaction with her parents when she was in college. In that case, you could say, "I remember you shared about a fight you had with your parents in college that seemed formative. How do you think that plays into your frustration with them now?"

Following up also helps your mentee reflect and evaluate life in a broader context than simply dealing with all the immediate tensions. Instead of just talking about "this week's irritations," proper follow-up makes sure issues are being worked out, and your mentee is gaining tools to interact with tensions in a more godly way. If, in our example, the follow-up from the frustration with the parents is now resolved, you can ask: "Why is it better?" "Was the issue ever addressed? Why or why not?" "What changed in you? In them?" "How do you avoid this in the future?" Without follow up, you would just hear about the latest issues and thoughts, never processing growth opportunities more fully.

Follow Through

The idea of mentorship is something that most people think is great, knowing it would be very beneficial. Yet, I've seen a vast disconnect between the concept of mentorship and the actual commitment to mentorship. As you begin to mentor others, you may think, "If they really want to be mentored, they would be the one reaching out to me, setting up the meeting, and making sure I remember."

In my experience, the more mature believer (you) should take on the responsibility of pursuing the mentee and setting up the meeting times. You can't force anyone to be mentored, but I've found that although people want mentoring, the excuses, busyness, and distraction of life gnaw away at its benefits. Being the one who always sets up the meetings does not necessarily mean you are doing a bad job or that you're not wanted as a mentor.

I see it this way: I take my daughters on a "daddy-daughter date" a few times a year. They love every date and "can't wait for next time," yet I find myself scheduling it each time. I could say to them, "Listen, if you really loved your daddy-daughter dates, then you'd be asking me to go on another one and follow up with me to make it happen." Even though the daddy-daughter date is really for their benefit, I don't get offended or annoyed they don't get out a calendar and ask, "When are we doing this next?" If they ever did, awesome, but being older, knowing the benefit to them, and loving them, I take on the responsibility of pursuing these dates. In the same way, pursue a relationship with your mentee. Follow through with scheduling each meeting date. Work to make it work, again and again.

When It Doesn't Work Out

There will be times when things don't work out. It could be for several reasons, including personality differences, time conflicts, disinterest in growth, or life circumstances. Whatever the case, when it doesn't work out, don't give up, and keep loving to learn.

1. Don't Give up.

Jesus also didn't say, "Go and make disciples, except if it doesn't work out with one, or a few, then at least you've given it a shot. You can quit." God knows people are difficult and relationships are hard, yet He still calls you to invest in others. Mentorship that doesn't work out can be very painful, but don't let the pain, frustration, or annoyance convince you to give up on the calling God has placed in your life.

2. Love to learn.

Perhaps your mentoring didn't work out because you didn't listen well. Maybe it was because you came down too hard in critiquing your mentee, or you hurt his feelings. I know it hurts to hear but be willing to seek honest feedback so you can make improvements. If your mentee says he doesn't want to meet with you anymore, swallow your pride and lovingly ask, "How could I have been a better mentor?" or "Was there anything I could have done differently?" You may have to press into this a little, as the first answer to this question is usually not the real answer. People won't want to offend you, but digging deeper, you may learn where you can grow, or you may learn that the breakdown had nothing to do with you. Take what he says, evaluate it for truth, and as much as it may hurt, love that you learned a bit about how to be a better mentor.

Replicating Mentorship

There will come a time in your mentorship when you feel like your mentee is ready to mentor others. In general, this happens sooner than you expect, sooner than they expect. Mentoring others isn't only for the spiritually elite, for those who have it all together. First, no one has it all together. Second, God has empowered every believer with the Holy Spirit. He has given every believer spiritual gifts to build up the church into the unity and likeness of Christ. Not just the 'spiritual leaders'—every person. Jesus calls all His disciples to invest in the lives of others, which means if you are mentoring a follower of Christ, they are called to invest in others too. Make sure that your mentorship challenges your mentee to mentor others. If they are scared because of a lack of understanding, remind them of this: If they have a heart for Christ, the Bible to guide them, a willingness to grow, and a supportive community (including you), they have all the tools needed. Also, remind them they can use this book as a guide to their mentoring.

> *Make sure that your mentorship challenges your mentee to mentor others.*

As you mentor, as they mentor, you will find one of the most significant growth opportunities actually occurs when you mentor others. There is a saying in the teaching world: "You don't know it till you teach it." I pray that as you mentor others toward Christ, you will come to know Him more, and those you mentor will apply the wisdom and love you've given them to go and do likewise—making disciples of all nations, baptizing them in the name of the Father, Son, and Holy Spirit.

Who are you mentoring?

Questions For Reflection:

- Who is someone in your life who asks great questions? What is that makes them great question askers?

- How do you feel after you've talked to that person? Why is that?

- How are you with asking questions, and what can you do to improve?

- Does asking tough questions come easy to you, or is it difficult? Why do you think that is?

- Where might your "curse of knowledge" affect your mentorship? What can you do to fight it?

- What do you like to do in your free time or what do you enjoy that you may be able to invite someone you're mentoring to do along with you?

- How do you typically deal with silence in a conversation?

- Between follow up and follow through: which is more difficult for you? Why? What can you do to improve on each of these?

- Who might God be calling you to pour into?

Chapter 23

Evangelism

After my hockey game, I sat at the bar, my stomach in knots, and my heart in my throat. Across from me was one of my teammates. He was sharing about his life, some of his struggles, and seemed to be seeking advice. I knew this was an opportunity to talk about my faith, about Jesus, but the concerns of what he may think and the fears of using the wrong words or sounding stupid were telling me to avoid any talk about God.

If there is one area of fully living out faith which brings the most hesitancy, it is the responsibility to evangelize. Evangelism is just a fancy word for talking to people about Jesus and inviting them to follow Him. Sharing your faith with Christians can be easy and enjoyable. Sharing your faith with those who don't hold your beliefs can be anxiety-filled and is often silenced by fear. This nervousness frequently arises from these three thoughts:

1. "How is the other person going to react?"

2. "What if they ask a question I can't answer?"

3. "What if I say the wrong thing?"

The bad news is all these fears are schemes of the devil to keep you from participating in expanding God's Kingdom—and they are effective. The good news is that when you understand your role and God's role in evangelism and what evangelism can be, those fears are revealed for what they are: silly little insecurities.

God's Role

God is the one who will change hearts, not you. In his letter to the church in Corinth, Paul makes this abundantly clear. "I planted the seed in your hearts, and Apollos watered it, but it was God who made it grow. It's not important who does the planting, or who does the watering. What's important is that God makes the seed grow" (1 Cor. 3:6-7). This statement is an affirmation of what Jesus said during His ministry, "But in fact, it is best for you that I go away, because if I don't, the Advocate won't come. If I do go away, then I will send him to you. And when he comes, he will convict the world of its sin, and of God's righteousness, and of the coming judgment. The world's sin is that it refuses to believe in me. Righteousness is available because I go to the Father, and you will see me no more. Judgment will come because the ruler of this world has already been judged" (Jn. 16:7-11).

The first step to silencing your fear is realizing God is the one who does the transformative work. This doesn't mean you have no role to play, as we'll see in the next section. It does mean if your fear is, "I don't

> *The first step to silencing your fears is realizing God is the one who does the transformative work.*

know the right things to say and I don't have all the answers," you can lay aside those worries. Your best knowledge and arguments aren't going to convince anyone to follow Christ. It also means if the person you are talking to rejects you, he isn't rejecting you. He is rejecting Jesus. You do have a role in evangelism, but every moment of your evangelism needs to be done with a desperation for God, not self-dependence on what "you" can accomplish.

With that said, it should be reassuring and inspiring to know that the Holy Spirit is a missionary Spirit. God desires to draw others to Him. God the Father, God the Son, and God the Holy Spirit are a single, trinitarian God. While they manifest in different ways, each aspect of the Trinity reflects the other two. When we look at God the Father, we see His ultimate sacrifice for us, out of love. When we look at Jesus, we see a pursuing God—a God who gave up His eternal authority to become a man—a God who took the form of a servant, living a perfect life, becoming the complete, undeserved sacrifice for you and me. Jesus shows us that God is not a passive, selective God. John 3:16 says, "For God so loved the world that He gave his one and only Son, that whoever believes in Him shall not perish, but have eternal life." (NIV) What you see in Jesus is God's loving pursuit of humanity. What you see in the Holy Spirit is the empowerment from God to work through you, to guide you to lovingly pursue others.

When you choose to follow Christ, you receive His Holy Spirit, who desires the world to know and accept His love. If God's pursuing Spirit is in you, there should be at least a rumbling desire in your soul to share God's love with others. That rumbling is not just a desire; it is the very power of God in you!

Your Role

Knowing God is in control and is working through you is a great comfort, but my guess is there is still some lingering fear. Understanding your role in evangelism can unleash you from that fear.

Prayer

Your first role in evangelism is prayer. If you aren't praying, then you're not relying on God to do the work. If you aren't relying on God to do the work, you are taking on the responsibility of something which is impossible for you to accomplish. Pray for specific people by name, to accept and follow Jesus. Pray for yourself—for an awareness of the opportunities God will give you to speak to others about Him. Pray for the courage to tell them about God's love and sacrifice. Pray for the Holy Spirit to speak through you as you interact with them. As we talked about in the chapter on prayer, prayer aligns your heart with God's, and God's heart is to make His love known.

Pointing Out The Obvious

One of the most helpful realizations I've had in silencing my fears of evangelism is that I'm merely pointing out the obvious. I have to admit, for most of my life I saw evangelism as "convincing from the absurd." I didn't have that name for it, but I basically thought, "I know you think this 'Jesus thing' is crazy, but hear me out; let me try to convince you it's something you should change your life for." Not only does that perspective make for an extremely unconvincing proposal, but it also puts a TON of responsibility on me to know all the ins and outs of theology, other religions, and all the objections someone might have.

Maybe this is how you've thought of evangelism, and it's driven you away from sharing about Christ. Here's the thing-as a believer in Christ, you are presenting the obvious truth, and their lack of belief is 'the absurd.' In the book of Romans, Paul says, "For ever since the world was created, people have seen the earth and sky. Through everything God made, they can clearly see his invisible qualities—his eternal power and divine nature. So they have no excuse for not knowing God." (Rm. 1:20).

> *As a believer in Christ, you are presenting the obvious truth, and a lack of belief is 'the absurd.'*

Did you hear that? If you are following Christ, it's because you've responded to the obvious. If anyone should be timid about their faith, it is those who place their faith in the absence of God. This verse isn't just encouragement in your faith. It is an encouragement in your evangelism. For me, this means when I talk about God and what Jesus has done in my life, I shouldn't worry if people think I'm crazy (although I definitely still struggle with that thinking). I should think they are crazy for not believing. Now, when I talk about Jesus, I'm less timid and much more matter of fact. After all, God's divine power and nature are obviously all around us. The confidence this perspective change brings doesn't mean that you should walk around with an air of cocky arrogance. It does mean that when you talk about Jesus, you can be settled that you aren't trying to "convince from the absurd," you are simply "pointing out the obvious."

You May Not Have The Gift, And That's Okay

Every Christian is called to be an evangelist, right? Wrong. Well...every Christian is called to evangelize, right? Well...Not exactly in the way you're probably thinking. In his letter to the church in Ephesus, Paul explains some of the different gifts Jesus has given to the church to build God's Kingdom. "Now these are the gifts Christ gave to the church: the apostles, the prophets, the evangelists, and the pastors and teachers…" (Eph. 4:11). I think you would agree that not everyone has the gift of teaching, and not everyone is an apostle. Now, how did you answer the question about evangelism at the beginning of the paragraph? If you said "yes, every Christian is called to be an evangelist," why evangelism different from the other gifts? There are apostles. There are prophets. Prophets aren't necessarily apostles, nor are apostles prophets. There are evangelists. There are shepherds. Evangelists aren't necessarily shepherds, nor shepherds evangelists. You get the point. Some people are gifted with evangelism, you may not be, and that's okay.

In fact, in another letter, Paul (the same author you just read) says:

"But we don't need to write to you about the importance of loving each other, for God himself has taught you to love one another. Indeed, you already show your love for all the believers throughout Macedonia. Even so, dear brothers and sisters, we urge you to love them even more. Make it your goal to live a quiet life, minding your own business and working with your hands, just as we instructed you before. Then people who are not believers will respect the way you live, and you will not need to depend on others" (1 Thess. 4:9-12).

Can you believe that? Paul tells them to live quietly and mind their own affairs. That seems to be in stark contrast to the idea that every believer should be an evangelist. You may have the gift of evangelism, and if you do, let me encourage you to use your gift as passionately and frequently as you can. Let me beg you to use your gift to help others reach people in their realm of influence. The church needs more evangelists sharing the Good News and training others to do the same. If you don't have the gift, well, not everyone is called to be an evangelist. But don't miss the truth that there is a calling on your life you can't ignore. The way you live, the way you interact with others, and the way you love should have an evangelizing effect.

You Still Have A Responsibility To Evangelize—It Just May Look Different Than You Think

You may not have a passion and a skill for sharing the Good News with those in your life. However, you still have a responsibility to interact with the world differently, in a way that reflects Jesus and shines a light into the

> *The way you live, the way you interact with others, and the way you love should have an evangelizing effect.*

darkness. The command Paul gives those he told to "live a quiet life, minding your own affairs" is to love in such a way, live in such a way, and work in such a way that others see Christ in you. Jesus calls every one of His followers to love God with all their heart, soul, and mind and to love others in the same way. (see Mt. 22:37-38)

The kind of love Jesus calls you to goes well beyond worldly, convenient love. Christian love should be radical, sacrificial, pursuant, Christ-based love. This type of love, in practice, is the basis of evangelism. As Jesus came into history, His religious community was looking for a kick-butt, destroy the enemy ruler. Jesus showed the world a different way, a way that got Him crucified, a way that changed history. The evangelism of Jesus wasn't contained to only His words. Jesus' evangelism was incorporated into His love, His atoning death, and His triumphant resurrection.

Evangelism doesn't only look like starting a "faith conversation" with someone sitting next to you on an airplane. It also appears as a pursuing, serving, Christ-like love toward those around you, ready to talk about Jesus when the opportunity comes. You may not be an "evangelist," but you are called to evangelize by living full of grace and truth, overflowing with compassion and godly love, and prepared to give an answer for the hope that you have.

Your call to evangelize doesn't stop at a profound love. You are also called to use your words to speak loving truth to others. Paul challenged his readers to use their words to reflect God's love and character. "Let no corrupting talk come out of your mouths, but only such as is good for building up, as fits the occasion, that it may give grace to those who hear" (Eph. 4:29, ESV).

Peter, another apostle, reminds his readers that God can give you a chance to evangelize at any moment, so be ready. "In your hearts revere Christ as Lord. Always be prepared to give an answer to everyone who asks you to give the reason for the hope that you have. But do this with gentleness and respect" (1 Pt. 3:15, NIV). Even though you may not have the gift of evangelism, if you live a life full of Christ-like love, there will be opportunities to share the Gospel with those in your life. Be ready to talk about who Jesus is, what He means to you, and let others know His gift is available for them. Your love is the foundation of evangelism, but don't dismiss the opportunities to talk about Jesus because "I'm just loving them." True love speaks the truth, lovingly. To not share about the salvation and hope that comes from trusting God is like being in a house fire with someone and thinking, "I don't need to tell them about the exits. I'm just going to hug them and show them how much I care." It's great that you want to show love, but true love would also show them the way to eternal life.

> *Your love is the foundation of evangelism, but don't dismiss the opportunities to talk about Jesus because "I'm just loving them." True love speaks the truth, lovingly.*

So, pray for those you know to be responsive to the Gospel. Pray for an opportunity to talk about Jesus. Pray for God's strength to align your life, love, and language to reflect the holy, loving perfection of God. Then live the life you just prayed for and be ready to respond to the opportunities God gives you.

How To Evangelize

Outside of what I just said about how you live, there are a ton of video and book resources on the internet which can give you hours of insight on how to evangelize. If that is something you're interested in, I cheer you on in your endeavor (just be sure that you put into practice what you learn and don't become a lame expert.) For our time, I'll quickly provide the easiest way to evangelize. I'm not doing this for the sake of disinterest, but because I think it's also the most natural and comfortable way.

Building friendships, not just acquaintances, with people God has placed in your life is the best way to evangelize. According to Amanda Haworth, "A person is your acquaintance if you only see them coincidentally instead of making intentional plans to see each other."[1] Conversations with an acquaintance usually revolve around quick, surface-level topics (politics, work, the kids, the weather). Acquaintances are not people with whom you discuss personal details or serious subjects. Sadly, we live in a time where most people's good friends are, at best, only acquaintances. As unfortunate as that is, it gives you a unique opportunity to show differentiating love by pursuing a deeper relationship. If most people's friends are "acquaintances," then most people lack personal, serious, caring conversations. If you aren't building deeper friendships, you can't expect to have meaningful, and possibly evangelistic, conversations.

Sometimes the fear of sharing about Jesus comes from the idea that you have to dive right in and make a plea for them to change everything about their life. Maybe God will call you to do that, but I think most of the time, He calls you to first build a loving relationship. What if, instead of worrying about "how to bring Jesus up in a discussion," you spent time getting to know someone in a way that would allow you to naturally talk about your own life... which should include Jesus.

Basically, be intentional with your relationships. Intentionality doesn't mean you have a hidden agenda of getting them to say "yes" to Jesus. You should desire for them to make the decision for Jesus, but if the intention of your relationship is simply to "make a convert," then you don't have the right perspective. Intentionality starts with care and says, "I really want to know you and serve you." You don't have to say that, but your actions, attitudes, and conversations do. Intentionality doesn't just talk about the latest sporting events, and it doesn't settle for "I'm fine." It lovingly seeks 'more' in order to hold their burdens with them, to share their joys, to provide a shoulder to cry on, to fuel the celebrations, to silence the insecurities, to provide a light in the darkness, and to remind them of hope. Intentionality sees them as image-bearers of a God who would leave the ninety-nine to go find the one. (see Mt. 18:12-14)

As you pour into those whom God has placed in your life, don't be ashamed to share your story, your struggles, and what God means to you. Intentionality looks for ways to move the conversation deeper. For most people, hearing about some

> *Intentionality sees others as image-bearers of a God who would leave the ninety-nine to go find the one.*

stories written in an ancient book they don't believe in doesn't draw them to a more in-depth discussion. Sharing how Jesus has changed and continues to affect your life is usually a better starting point. This is because it's personal to you and they can hopefully see the difference He's made in your life by the way you've loved and cared for them. If sharing your story doesn't produce a conversation about faith, that's alright. Remember Paul's words, "I planted... Apollos watered... but God made it grow" (1 Cor. 3:6). You may just be planting seeds, and God can take your story and allow it to grow to a curiosity later on.

On the other hand, you may feel prompted by their reaction or by the Holy Spirit to dig a little deeper and talk specifically about faith. If that's the case, here are some intentional questions:

Where are you spiritually?

What do you think of my story?

Have you ever thought about faith?

What are your biggest objections to Jesus?

Pay attention to their disposition as you ask these questions because you want to be sure you're not making them feel like they are a 'project' to you. Again, your motivation should be centered on loving and caring for them, with a desire that they come to know Jesus, not the other way around.

Intentionality, in your conversations and actions, should reflect God's pursuant, caring love. When you do this with prayer, ready to respond to the Holy Spirit, He will give you opportunities to evangelize. When that time comes, by the Spirit's power, with the confidence that you're just pointing out the obvious, and with the knowledge that it is God who does the work—share unashamedly.

In my conversation with my teammate, I used these very tools to help me silence my fears and speak freely about my faith and the difference God has made in my life. As is always the case when I fought through my insecurities to talk about Jesus, the conversation was way less intimidating than I expected, much better received, and I left excited that I was able to share the ultimate, eternal truth with someone I cared about. Though he didn't come to a saving faith in Jesus at that moment, I continue to pray that my willingness to evangelize planted a seed which God will cultivate and grow into a life of faith.

<u>Questions For Reflection:</u>

- Do you think you have the gift of evangelism? Why or why not?

- What makes you most nervous about sharing your faith? Why?

- Does "pointing out the obvious" help reframe how you approach evangelism? Talk about that.

- Who are three people you will be praying for, asking God for the opportunity to develop an intentional relationship?

- What was most helpful in this chapter for you?

- What did God stir in you as you read this?

Conclusion

Live it Out!

As I said at the beginning of this book, "You don't have to be an expert to fully live out your faith." All the insight you've gained from these chapters must move you to the action of developing your relationship with God and using your life to show others the truth of Jesus. The intention of giving you an overview of the basics (and not so basics) of Christianity wasn't so that you would be a smarter Christian, with more information, but to silence the lies of:

"I just don't understand enough."

"I've got too many questions."

"I'm not as smart as..."

"I need more information before I start to live fully for Christ, pouring into others..." or whatever other lie may be keeping you from fully living out your faith.

I'm sure this book hasn't settled all your fears. I'm confident you have more questions (and more questions are good). Still, I hope it has enriched your understanding of God, the Bible, and Christianity in a way that moves you to put your faith into action.

I pray you have been equipped to move beyond this book to a fuller appreciation of the amazing grace of God, the beauty of His plan, and a more profound sense of His love. I pray you now are eager to take what you've learned and pour into others. I pray this is a springboard to developing your relationship with God and using your life to serve Him and serve others. As you've learned about each topic, I hope you've gained the confidence to love boldly, serve regularly, mentor others, and share the Good News of Jesus Christ.

May you be reminded that above all the knowledge you've gained, God's Holy Spirit is in you. With His power, you can participate in changing lives for His glory! There is no need to be paralyzed by your fears anymore. Be confident of God's power and presence in you. Please, I beg you, don't take what you've learned and do nothing. Exercise your faith, involve yourself at church, serve and mentor others, use your life for His glory, and experience the thrill of fully living out your faith. Continue spending time in God's Word, in God's community, and in the things which spiritually fill you. As you take what you've learned and live more like Christ, you will discover the fullness of God's presence in your life will be more fully realized when you love, serve, disciple, and lay your life down for others.

I'd like to end your reading with one of my favorite benedictions, followed by another beautiful benediction I came across recently. I pray these two concluding statements will help launch you from everything you've received here to fully living out your faith.

"May God bless you with a restless *discomfort* about easy answers, half-truths, and superficial relationships, so that you may seek truth boldly and love deep within your heart.

May God bless you with holy *anger* at injustice, oppression, and exploitation of people, so that you may tirelessly work for justice, freedom, and peace among all people.

May God bless you with the gift of *tears* to shed for those who suffer from pain, rejection, starvation, or the loss of all that they cherish, so that you may reach out your hand to comfort them and transform their pain into joy.

May God bless you with enough *foolishness* to believe that you really can make a difference in this world, so that you are able, with God's grace, to do what others claim cannot be done." [1]

And...

"Remember, you will be nowhere by accident this week. Wherever you are, you will be there by the divine appointment of Almighty God. He will do His work through you this week. You will be His hands, His feet, His voice; because YOU are the salt of the earth, YOU are the light of the world, YOU are the hope of your community. Never allow the thought— 'I am of no use where I am'. You certainly are of no use where you are not. All you have to do is show up. God has already been where you will be!" [2]

Now...

Fully live out your faith!

Questions For Reflection:

- What do you need to do to make sure you don't fall back into the traps of your fears?

- Who can you call right now to help you continue to fully live out your faith?

- Who is someone you can take through this material to help them develop their understanding and faith?

Acknowledgments

I would like to acknowledge, with deep gratitude the following people for their influence on my life and their support of this book:

To Amy, I love you the most-est-er. You are amazing and there is so much you do for our family and for me that my appreciation for you will always be less than you deserve. For that I apologize, but I hope you know how eternally grateful I am for what you do, who you are, and your love for me. To my kids- Makenna, Bailey, Bryce, and Adeline- when you get older, you'll understand what I'm about to say. I can't believe you're my kids…like, you are MY kids. To be called "Daddy" by you is something I too often take for granted. I know there will be plenty of times when I misrepresent what the role of a Father looks like. I pray in those times, you would forgive me, and you would see the distance between the perfect Father and me exposes the truth of God's overwhelming goodness, grace, patience, and love. Thanks for all the laughter and joy you bring into my life. I'll love you no matter what.

To Kyle, when I ask other twins about their experience with their sibling, I find a range of answers that draw me to a deeper appreciation of you and a thankfulness for our relationship. You are my best friend (besides Amy) and have been a constant support in my life. Thanks for your love and friendship. To Heather, your prayers and encouragement have meant more than you know and I'm so grateful for you. To Josiah, Amanda, Janae, Will, Jenny, Grant, and Ashley, it's an honor to call you my brothers and sisters and to have the relationship we do despite the distance. To Bill and Jeni thank you for always supporting me, loving my family well, and taking a deep interest in the work I do. To Mom and Dad, there are so many things I've experienced as a parent which I've thought, "I had no idea how much Mom and Dad did." Your love, encouragement, and the ways you crafted our family's closeness to one another and God—all the things I thought were 'normal' I realize aren't as common as I thought—For all those things, thank you. Aunt Carol and Uncle Don thank you to for your genuine interest and care for me and my family and Aunt Carol thank you so much for all the editing you provided. Grandma, I know you're enjoying the presence of God, and I pray He relays this message- Thank you for ALL your prayers, your love and your example of steadfast and confident joy in the Lord. I miss you.

To Nathan Smith, Steve Clifford and Adam Miller thank you for seeing things in me I never knew were there, walking alongside me in my immaturity and growth to encourage me in ministry and life. To the group of pastors I meet with regularly- Eric, Chris, John, Robb- You have been a huge blessing in my life and I'm honored to call you friends! To Tom for your prayers, your heart for the Lord, your interest in my life and your friendship. To Brett I'd send a .gif of my thanks to you because you'd understand that better, but that doesn't work here, so imagine Dr. Evil with his arms open waving you in for a hug. To all those who offered input on the editing process you've helped craft this book to be so much better and I appreciate your honest and helpful feedback.

To Real Life elders, staff, and congregation, thank you for allowing me the opportunity to lead you. I love you, and I pray we would be a people who are desperately dependent on God, making Jesus > everything, and that through your time in this community you would come to embrace fully living out your faith.

Resource Page

Drew Froese Speaking and Blog

www.drewfroese.com

Bible Reading

Dr. Tom Constable www.soniclight.com

The Bible Project www.thebibleproject.com

Spiritual Gifts Test

https://gifts.churchgrowth.org/spiritual-gifts-survey/

https://spiritualgiftstest.com

https://giftstest.com

Continued Recommended Reading

How to Read the Bible for All it's Worth Fee and Stuart

Celebration of Discipline Richard Foster

Mere Christianity C.S. Lewis

Cost of Discipleship Bonhoeffer

Knowledge of the Holy A.W. Tozer

Endnotes

Introduction

[1] Tozer, A.W., "give Time to God," in *Mornings with Tozer: Daily Devotional Readings* (Chicago: Moody Publishers, 2015) reading for February 24.

Chapter 1

[1] Lifeway Research (2017, May 19). Episode 16: *Americans Like the Bible More Than They Read It* [Audio podcast]. https://lifewayresearch.com/2017/05/19/episode-16-americans-like-the-bible-more-than-they-read-it/.

Chapter 2

[1] Roat, A. (2020, June 22) *What is Biblical Hermeneutics and Is it Still Important Today?* Christianity.com. https://www.christianity.com/wiki/bible/meaning-origin-history-of-biblical-hermeneutics.html

Chapter 3

[1] Nässelqvist, D., & Jardim, G. (2016). Slavery. In J. D. Barry, D. Bomar, D. R. Brown, R. Klippenstein, D. Mangum, C. Sinclair Wolcott, … W. Widder (Eds.), *The Lexham Bible Dictionary*. Bellingham, WA: Lexham Press.

[2] Lewis, C. S., *Surprised by Joy* (Harcourt, Brace, Jovanovich, 1966) ch. 13, pp. 207-8

Chapter 4

[1] Piper, J (2008, Sept. 20) *In The Beginning was the Word. https://www.*

Chapter 5

[1] Barnett, J (2010, Aug 31) *Four Gospels, Four Audiences?* From *"The Gospels in Harmony"* (Discover the book Ministries). https://www.christianity.com/jesus/is-jesus-god/the-gospels/four-gospels-four-audiences.html

Chapter 9

[1] Tozer, A.W. *The Set of the Sail.* (Wingspread, New edition, 2007)

[2] Webster, N. (1828). *An American dictionary of the English language: intended to exhibit, I. The origin, affinities and primary signification of English words, as far as they have been ascertained; II. the genuine orthography and pronunciation of words, according to general.* S. Converse, Printed by Hezekiah Howe).

[3] Kennebrew, D (2012, Nov 6) *What is true worship?* Christianitytoday.com. https://www.christianitytoday.com/biblestudies/bible-answers/spirituallife/what-is-true-worship.html

[4] Graham, Billy (n.d.) goodreads.com. https://www.goodreads.com/quotes/7237162-the-highest-form-of-worship-is-the-worship-of-unselfish

Chapter 10

[1] Kelly, T. *A Testament of Devotion* (HarperOne, 1996)

[2] Foster, R. *Celebration Of Discipline* (New York: Harper & Row, 1978)

[3] Kierkegaard, S. *Christian Discourses: The Crisis and a Crisis in the life of an actress.* (Princeton University Press, 1997)

Chapter 11

[1] Strong, J. (2009). *A Concise Dictionary of the Words in the Greek Testament and The Hebrew Bible* (Vol. 2, p. 32). Bellingham, WA: Logos Bible Software.

[2] "Meditate." https://www.vocabulary.com/dictionary/meditate

[3] Kelsey, M. *The Other Side of Silence* (New York, Paulist Press, 1997)

[4] Foster, R. *Celebration Of Discipline* (New York: Harper & Row, 1978.)

[5] Bonhoeffer, D. *Life Together* (Fortress Press, 2015)

Chapter 12

[1] Logos Bible Software *Bible Sense Lexicon* (Faithlife Corporation 2000-2021)

[2] Nee, W. *The Spiritual Man.* (Christian Fellowship Publishers, 1968)

Chapter 19

[1] Strong, J. (2009). *A Concise Dictionary of the Words in the Greek Testament and The Hebrew Bible* (Vol. 1, p. 45). Bellingham, WA: Logos Bible Software.

Chapter 21

[1] Keller, T. *Romans 1-7 For You.* (The Good Book Company, 2014)

Chapter 22

[1] Heath, C; Heath, D. *Made to Stick.* (Random House, 2007)

Chapter 23

[1] Haworth, A. *Acquaintance vs Friend- Definition (With Examples).* Socialpronow.com. https://socialpronow.com/blog/difference-friend-acquaintance/ (2018, March 13)

Conclusion

[1] Fox, Sister Ruth. *The Origin of "A Franciscan Prayer- a Non-Traditional Blessing.* Gingerling.co.uk. http://www.gingerling.co.uk/the-origin-of-a-franciscan-prayer-a-non-traditional-blessing/ (2019, Aug 28)

[2] Dick, P. *Thank You.* 633seekfirst.wordpress.com. https://633seekfirst.wordpress.com/2013/12/30/thank-you/ (2013, Dec 30)